THE BUG BOOK

A FLY FISHER'S GUIDE TO TROUT STREAM INSECTS

PAUL WEAMER

The Bug Book
Fly Fisher's Guide to Trout Stream Insects
Paul Weamer
Headwater Books
Copyright © 2017 by Headwater Books LLC

Published by

HEADWATER
BOOKS

Headwater Books
PO Box 202
Boiling Springs, PA 17007
www.headwaterbooks.com

Printed in India
First edition
ISBN: 978-1-934753-42-2
eBook ISBN: 978-1-934753-37-8
Cover and interior design by Gavin Robinson

10 9 8 7 6 5 4

Library of Congress Control Number: 2016941916

CONTENTS

DEDICATION

To Dakota, Brandy, Grizzly, and Midge the Mastiff . . .
best friends.

ACKNOWLEDGMENTS

Thanks to Ross Purnell and *Fly Fisherman* magazine for allowing me to write about bugs for the best fly-fishing periodical in the world.

Thanks to Orvis, Simms, Regal Engineering, Montana Fly Company, and Daiichi.

Thanks to TCO, West Branch Anglers, Border Water Outfitters, Mutton Hollow Outfitters, and the Dette Fly Shop.

Thanks to Dan Gigone and Sweetwater Fly Shop in Livingston, Montana, for your support.

Thanks to Greg Hoover and Charlie Meck for all the time you've spent discussing bugs with me.

Thanks to my excellent editor and publisher, Jay Nichols, for your many great ideas, allowing me to borrow a couple of your bug photos, and for years of friendship.

Thanks to my wife, Ruthann, for your never-ending assistance and for encouraging me to shoot photographs and write this book.

INTRODUCTION

A trout-like view from beneath a mayfly spinner. Trout use light from the sky, even at night, combined with their terrific vision, to scrutinize aquatic insects before eating them off the water's surface. This selectivity is one of the reasons that trout are so fun to catch.

There is a reason why we fly anglers call all of our hand-tied lures, even big streamers tied to imitate baitfish, flies. At its heart, fly fishing is, and has always been, a sport where bits of hair and feathers are tied to hooks to imitate insects that are being eaten by trout. Modern fly anglers now pursue just about any fish species that swims, but fly fishermen have always cast flies to trout. And more often than you might realize, it was adventurous, former match-the-hatch trout fishermen who first explored warmwater and saltwater venues.

Do you need to understand aquatic insect hatches to catch trout? Not really. European nymphing techniques have become popular and effective in recent years, and many of the practitioners with whom I've spoken have limited understandings of aquatic insects. Streamer fishing is also currently experiencing a popularity boom, and you don't need to know anything about insects if your main goal is to imitate baitfish. So why should any trout fisherman learn about hatches?

Understanding aquatic insect hatches is like being able to cast an entire fly line. Do you need to cast that far to catch fish? Of course not. But will being able to cast a long distance inhibit your ability to catch fish? Never. Knowing where, and how, insects live and emerge gives anglers yet another piece of the puzzle. I've never heard a fly

Unknown to science before the 1980s, this *Heptagenia culacantha* mayfly dun is one of the largest in the United States. I found and photographed this one on the Delaware River's main stem above Callicoon, New York.

fisherman exclaim, "I probably would have caught those rising fish if I just didn't know so much about trout stream insects."

You still need to cast. You still need to present flies in such a manner that fish will accept them. But though no one has ever failed to catch a trout because they knew too much about aquatic insects, plenty of anglers have not caught as big a fish, or as many fish as they could have caught, because they failed to understand the importance of matching a hatch. This is particularly true when fishing for large, wild, selective trout—the ones we all really want to catch.

And there's another important reason to pay attention to aquatic insects: They are fascinating. Anglers miss so much of the natural world's wonder when they ignore the bugs. Mayflies are beautiful in their brief lives, attempting to perpetuate their species against great odds, just as they've done for thousands of years. They come in amazing colors, in many sizes, and they sometimes present unexpected mysteries.

One of the largest mayflies in North America, *Heptagenia culacantha*, was discovered in the 1980s in Pennsylvania's Susquehanna River near Three Mile Island. That's amazing! How many other living creatures in the United States are so mysterious and unknown that they are yet to be discovered? And entomologists today believe that there are hundreds of aquatic insect species yet to be discovered. We anglers have a front row seat to this unknown world every time we go fishing.

When I was first learning to fly fish, I found the complicated Latin names and life stages of aquatic insects very confusing. It was as if the whole fly fishing world was born knowing about these things, and I was left out. In this book, I try to relieve some of the reticence about trout stream insects that makes many anglers feel inadequate and uneasy. Many excellent books have been written that provide very detailed information about many different hatches. But that's not this book's goal. This book is written for new anglers who want a basic understanding of aquatic insects and which hatches are most important. Or for more seasoned fly fishers who want to take their skills to the next level; those who want to know not only *if* their flies will work but *why* they'll work as well. This book's aim is to provide basic aquatic insect knowledge that will not only help you to understand more about trout stream insects, but it will also help you catch more trout on your next fishing trip. It will help you to understand why you should tie one fly to your leader rather than another to imitate the hatches you encounter.

I begin Chapter 1 by looking at the different types of aquatic habitats—rivers, streams, and stillwaters—where aquatic insects reside. Each of these habitats provides very specific conditions that make some aquatic insects thrive and others fail. This has a tremendous impact on the food available to the fish and what you need to be imitating to catch them. In Chapter 2, I help clarify trout stream insect names. Most new fly anglers, and many old ones, struggle to understand common and scientific aquatic insect names, and why they always seem to be changing. This chapter explains why it's important to understand these names and how they work.

Chapters 3, 4, and 5 discuss the big three aquatic insect families—mayflies, caddisflies, and stoneflies—the most important types of trout stream insects in the United States. Understanding these major aquatic insect groups is the key to putting more fish in your net.

Chapter 6 includes a series of three Hatch Progression and Importance Charts, which outline the order in which hatches occur and their respective importance to anglers throughout the country. These charts will cut through the hundreds of possible mayflies, caddisflies, and stoneflies that live in North American waters to get to the ones that really matter for fishing. I use the Mississippi River as the dividing line between the East/Midwest and West because aquatic insect species really begin to differ from a continental perspective nearest this geographical feature. Although it is important to realize that there are also continent-wide, overlapping species.

The charts not only highlight important families and species throughout the United States but also the most angler-important life stages for each insect. I use a 1 to 5 ranking system for all the charts, where 1 is equivalent to poor and 5 is excellent. These rankings give you an idea of what you can expect to be happening on the water and

It's a trout's tendency to rise for dry flies that makes it special to fly fishers. All trout species eat insects from the water's surface: browns, brooks, rainbows, cutthroat, and this cutthroat/rainbow hybrid, known as a cuttbow, caught by Ruthann Weamer in Yellowstone National Park's Lamar River.

help give you a game plan before you get to the water. The chapter ends with a brief look at phenology, which is the study of the relationship between plant and animal cycles. Did you know that you can often predict what is hatching on your favorite trout stream by looking at the plants blooming in your yard?

Chapter 7 examines how to choose the proper fly pattern to imitate hatch stages. It ties together the aquatic insect information found in chapters 3 through 5 to fly patterns and fishing techniques that are most effective for imitating them. The chapter begins with a look at trigger mechanisms, masking hatches, and drag: three important topics for making sure that your fly patterns really are imitating the aquatic insects you find. A closer look at specific dry flies, wet flies, nymphs, and emergers then follows. The patterns included will catch trout from Maine to Oregon and all points in between.

Chapters 8 and 9 profile the best hatches in the country by once again dividing the United States into East/Midwest and West regions. Each of the hatches highlighted in this chapter received at least two five star ratings in Chapter 6's Hatch Progression Charts. That means that two or more of their life stages are of the highest importance to fly fishing. A photograph and brief synopsis are included for each five star hatch.

Finally, chapter 10 examines lesser known aquatic insects and land-dwelling terrestrials, which I call "Other Insects," that can also be very important for catching trout, sometimes even more important than mayflies, caddisflies, and stoneflies. This chapter also includes a final chart, comprised with the same 1 to 5 ranking scale I used in the previous charts, showing the importance of these "other" insects for anglers across North America.

The book ends with some selective reading options for Eastern/Midwestern and Western anglers. If what you read in these chapters interests you, and you want to learn even more, then the suggested books and websites I've listed will help you do that. But one of the best ways to learn is to spend time streamside, looking at the bugs, trying different fly patterns, and catching fish. So make sure you do that as much as you can. Good luck!

1

AQUATIC INSECT HABITATS

Montana's Yellowstone River begins as a typical Western freestone river in Yellowstone National Park. Native cutthroat trout are most common in the river's coldest upper sections, but as the river flows and warms, rainbows and eventually brown trout become the most commonly caught species. All trout and aquatic insect species do not prefer the same water habitat or temperature.

A quatic insect hatch intensity and diversity is greatly influenced by the rivers, streams, lakes, and ponds in which they occur. There are five major types of fisheries where anglers pursue trout: freestone rivers and streams, tailwaters, limestone streams and spring creeks, rehabilitating rivers and streams, and stillwaters. Each one has its own subtleties that are important to understand if you want to catch the trout that reside in them. Certain insects find one or more of these habitats ideal while being less tolerant of others. There is a great deal of overlap, and some aquatic insects may be found in all water types, but there are specialists too. Some aquatic insects are more tolerant of pollution, and they'll be the first to reappear as a stream heals from toxins. Stoneflies aren't often found in stillwaters, but there is a mayfly species that only lives in this calm water. Some species thrive in the artificially cold environs of tailwaters, while others prefer warmer water. And some need the highly oxygenated flows from a bubbling freestoner while others bask in the nutrient-rich, but placid flows of a spring creek. Understanding the types of aquatic insects that are drawn to the various kinds of trout water will help better prepare you to imitate them with flies.

Most freestone rivers flowing from the Rocky Mountains begin as glacier or snowmelt streams. In their headwaters, these icy flows are low in nutrients but fairly stable with cold temperatures, creating specific habitats that are usually colonized by only a few aquatic insects. Because of this, the fish usually have little to eat, which often means there are fewer of them and they are smaller in size in the headwaters than the lower, warmer parts of the watershed.

FREESTONE RIVERS AND STREAMS

Most of the flowing waterways throughout the United States are classified as freestone rivers or streams. A freestone river or stream is a body of flowing water that is primarily fed by rainfall runoff or snowmelt and the acquired flows of other creeks and rivers. Freestone streams will also probably be fed by underground springs, but this is not their primary component.

Large freestone rivers, particularly those that course outside the range of high mountains like the Rockies, are generally the warmest bodies of flowing water in a region because they are often wide, allowing the sun to warm them, and because they are the culmination of other streams that have also warmed as they flowed. Aquatic insect hatches usually begin in the warmest, lower sections of freestone rivers and slowly work their way upstream, as the water warms, ending ultimately in their much colder, headwater tributaries.

Hatches begin in warmer waters because the insects require a certain number of days above a specific water temperature for their bodies to fully develop. The exact number of days and the exact temperature differs widely among aquatic insect species and the type of waters in which they live. So a Blue Winged Olive that lives in an always-cold tailwater river may develop at a different rate than the same insect living in a much more temperature variable freestone fishery.

Some Western freestone rivers are fed by great glaciers and snowfall originating high in the mountains. These rivers flow cold in their headwaters nearest the mountains, and they are often sterile because they are almost entirely composed of melt water. Water from melting snow has few nutrients for aquatic insect to feed upon so there is little biodiversity (differing species of aquatic insects) and less for trout to eat, often producing sparse hatches and small fish. But as these rivers flow from the mountains, they receive inflows from smaller tributaries that originate as spring creeks or freestone streams and their added fertility increases biodiversity, so aquatic insect populations and fish size increase.

Because elevation has such a dramatic effect on water temperature, Western hatches in the Rocky Mountain region's freestone rivers and streams will occur significantly later (up to a month or two) than the same hatches east or west of the mountains. Even in the East's much smaller Appalachian Mountains, elevation makes streams colder and hatches occur later than those in valley streams.

Many sections of freestone streams are often turbulent, which makes them ideal for aquatic insects that require the higher levels of oxygen generated as water tumbles over rocks. Stoneflies, many caddis species, and clinger mayfly nymphs that live predominately in riffled water are all common in freestone streams.

Freestoners also usually include the widest varieties of aquatic insects because these rivers and streams have the greatest habitat range, from brawling riffles or rapids to long, slow pools. They also include microhabitats such as pockets of slow water behind a boulder within a large riffle where sediment collects, providing a miniature habitat for burrowing mayflies. And wide temperature ranges from very cold to sometimes warm ensure that both cold- and warmwater aquatic insect species can find a spot to live.

But, though hatch variety is at its peak in a freestone river or stream, hatch intensity is usually lower. The sterile nature of freestone streams combined with ever-changing habitat usually means that no single species gains an overwhelming presence. Some freestone hatches can be intense, but it's more likely that throughout the season there will be many different insects hatching at the same time rather than one super-hatch.

TAILWATERS

If you build a dam on a river or stream and release water from it, you change that waterway into a tailwater. There are two types of tailwaters: Those that release cool or cold water from the bottom of the dam and those that release warmer water from levels higher in the dam. Some reservoirs are not deep enough to form a thermocline to shield the sun's rays and create a cold water region, so their releases are often warm no matter how high or low in the dam they occur. Deep lakes create a thermocline, a thin layer that separates warm water from cold water, and this keeps them very cold near their bottoms. This artificially cold water has a great impact on aquatic insect hatches.

Glacier and snowmelt streams such as Glacier National Park's McDonald Creek often flow crystal clear because they are low in nutrients. A greenish tint often indicates snowmelt in the stream.

New York's Upper Delaware, Montana's Bighorn, New Mexico's San Juan, Tennessee's South Holston, North Carolina's Hiwassee, and Arkansas' White are all cold, tailwater river fisheries created from deep lakes. But any kind of manmade water release, warm or cold, can completely throw the natural world out of whack, making hatch timing difficult to predict. In some of these fisheries, like the Upper Delaware River branches, releases are not predictable or steady. If a water release is greatly curtailed for an extended period, the river can warm unnaturally because its low flow is heated more easily by the sun, while freestone rivers in the area are running high from snowmelt or rain. This can accelerate the timing of an aquatic insect emergence in the tailwater.

Conversely, if a great deal of cold water is being released, then hatches can be suppressed. Unnatural amounts of cold water can even change the way an aquatic insect species lives. Little Sulphurs *(E. dorothea dorothea)* on the Delaware River tailwaters hatch all summer when cold water is released. They appear to produce multiple generations even though they are not known to do this in natural flowing streams. Multiple generations mean that the fertilized eggs from one set of male and female Sulphurs hatch and then mate and their offspring hatch again in the same year. This is common for some species like Blue Winged Olives *(Baetis* spp.) but not Sulphurs.

Tailwaters often have less aquatic insect diversity than freestoners, especially the closer you get to the reservoir. Areas nearest the water release point will be artificially cold and that will limit the species that can live there. However, this cold water does create optimum conditions for some species, and they can sometime hatch in incredible numbers for long periods of time. Sometimes, the tailwater's impoundment shields the waterway from floods and sediments accumulate as a result. This isn't good for the overall health of the system. But it can artificially inflate populations of certain types of aquatic insects such as burrowing mayflies that need sediments to create their burrows, while inhibiting others such as like clinger mayflies, which need water freely flowing through clean gravel, unimpeded by sediments, to survive.

LIMESTONE STREAMS AND SPRING CREEKS

Some of the United States' most famous and revered trout fisheries are classified as limestone streams or spring creeks. Montana's beautiful Paradise Valley streams—Armstrong's, Nelson's, DePuy's—and the Midwest's Driftless Area streams are classic examples of spring creeks as much as Pennsylvania's historic Big Spring and Letort are prototypical limestone streams. Spring creeks and limestone streams can be found across the United States.

Both of these stream types originate with underground springs. The primary difference is that limestone streams are often formed in areas of karst geology where acidic rainwater seeps into the ground through small cracks. The acidic water dissolves the alkaline limestone, reducing the water's pH. The water then carries the dissolved rock with it as it flows, and the limestone creates fertile conditions for aquatic insects, plant life, and trout.

Spring water, whether limestone influenced or not, maintains the mean temperature of the region in which it flows. There are limestone streams in Florida but they are too warm to harbor trout. In parts of the northern United States springs emerge from the ground near 50 degrees; perfect temperatures to ensure trout survival and growth.

Spring and limestone creeks are commonly known for their large populations of scuds and sow bugs. These small, freshwater crustaceans thrive in cold, placid waters with a high pH and can sometimes be found in staggering numbers, crawling or swimming amidst the vegetation. Trout love to eat them, and they grow big and fat by doing so.

Limestone streams and spring creeks are much closer to tailwaters than freestone streams in their aquatic insect composition because their placid currents and near constant water temperatures leave few areas for diversity that is needed by a wide range of insects. Swimming and burrowing mayflies are common as are caddisflies, but clinger mayflies and stoneflies are generally less common and less diversified in spring creeks.

New York and Pennsylvania's Upper Delaware River is one of the most famous tailwater trout fisheries in the country. Wild trout get large here by feeding on abundant aquatic insect hatches, in relatively stable environments, controlled by large dams.

Many northern trout fishermen may be surprised to learn that there are mayflies living in the Deep South's streams and lakes. This *Hexagenia orlando* male spinner emerged from a lake near Kissimmee, Florida.

Sadly, many of our country's historically best limestone and spring creeks have been diminished in modern times. The steady water flows and temperature make them ideal areas to build fish hatcheries. Hatchery effluent is toxic and its discharge has damaged many streams. Good farming land also accompanies many limestone and spring creeks because the streams lie in fertile valleys. And poor farming practices and pesticides have killed and diminished aquatic insect life in many streams. Pristine spring creeks have abundant, diverse aquatic insect hatches. But those that have been harmed by hatcheries, poor logging and farming practices, or other types of pollution, often do not.

REHABILITATING RIVERS AND STREAMS

Rivers and streams that are recovering from pollution are greatly limited in their aquatic insect diversity. Pollution can be caused by current and former mining or fracking operations, run off from agricultural fields or paved surfaces, pesticides leaking or leaching from industrial uses and homeowners, soil erosion from poor logging practices and road construction, or one-time catastrophic events like chemical spills from holding tanks or during tractor trailer or train accidents.

After a catastrophic pollution event, a river or stream will begin to heal simply by moving the toxins downstream with the natural flow of water. Heavy flow events like floods will further aid the extrication of toxins. But some streams, like those receiving constant in-flows of AMD (Acid Mine Drainage) water, can't really begin to heal until the underlying problem is fixed.

Sadly, some streams in my former home state of Pennsylvania are not expected to be healthy enough to sustain aquatic life for the next 10,000 years because of AMD. But some streams where mines have been sealed, or liming (the addition of limestone rock or sand) measures have been added, or where other factors have caused the cessation of the acid and heavy metals, are beginning to recover. And the same is true for many other streams across the country that have had hatches decimated by pollution that is no longer occurring or still occurring but at greatly reduced levels.

These streams will not have their full complement of possible hatches. But there are some aquatic insect species that seem better equipped to withstand some pollution, and they are the first to reappear as a stream heals. In the East, Big Sulphurs (*E. invaria*), Little Black Stoneflies (*Taeniopteryx* spp.), and Tan Caddis (*Hydropsyche* spp.) are often the first insects to return, though there are others.

Some streams like central Pennsylvania's Spring Creek have chemical pollutants that are ingrained into the streambed. This type of pollution is unrecoverable for some aquatic insect species. Forests that are cut down will regenerate. Wildflowers and native plants can often times be regrown once invasives have been removed. But if you allow a stream to be polluted, it may lose its hatches forever.

Spring and limestone creeks are often characterized by flat, slow-moving pools with weedy bottoms, perfect habitat for freshwater crustaceans and some mayfly species. The slow flows give fish ample time to scrutinize fly patterns, making them very challenging for fly fishers.

STILLWATERS: LAKES AND PONDS

A stillwater is a nonmoving body of water such as a pond or lake. Stillwaters are not often considered trout fisheries by Mid-Atlantic and southern U.S. trout fishers, though some impoundments in these regions do contain trout, most often through fish stocking programs. But anglers in New York's Adirondack region and in the New England states know the value of stillwaters from their many lakes and ponds where brook trout and landlocked salmon thrive. Perhaps there's an even greater appreciation for stillwaters in the western United States. Some of their fisheries are well known throughout fly fishing lore: Utah's Strawberry Reservoir, Colorado's Spinney Reservoir, Nevada's Pyramid Lake, the famed "gulpers" in Montana's Hebgen Lake, just to name a few, are nearly as famous as the great Western trout rivers.

Stillwaters often produce excellent hatches from midges, dragon and damselflies, and some mayfly and caddis species. Generally, stoneflies require cold moving water for their survival, so they are much less common in stillwaters. But some mayfly species that are not often common, or important, in flowing waters such as *Callibaetis* can be important in stillwater ponds or lakes.

Aquatic insect hatches and fishing in general is often more stable in stillwater fisheries because water level fluctuations are much less sudden or dramatic than they are in rivers and streams. I've had a couple fly fishing trips saved by non-planned detours to stillwater fisheries when water conditions were less than ideal on the river or stream I was supposed to fish.

Western fly fishermen are blessed with many scenic, trout-filled lakes and ponds. These fisheries should not be considered second rate when compared to rivers and streams. Many stillwaters contain wild fish and excellent hatches.

Callibaetis mayflies are often important hatches in stillwater fisheries. Some mayfly species are generalists, able to live in widely varied habitats. But the *Callibaetis* species are specialists, requiring still waters or large eddies and pond-like areas of rivers and streams.

2

THE NAME GAME:
LATIN VS. COMMON NAMES

The male Hendrickson dun (above) (*Ephemerella subvaria*) is easily differentiated from a female by the presence of its large, red eyes. The female Hendrickson's dark colored eyes are much smaller. When famed New York fly tier, Roy Steenrod, gave this mayfly its common name, and created his fly pattern to imitate it, he was referring only to the males.

M ost aquatic insects that are important to fly fishers are known by one or two scientific names (also called Latin names) and a common name. This is true for all three major aquatic insect types—mayflies, caddisflies, and stoneflies—though mayfly names are often more commonly known by anglers.

Scientific names are created by entomologists, and they most often stand for the name of a person who discovered or researched the insect, though sometimes they are derived from other sources such as mayfly family relationships. **Common names** are created by anglers. They're use is often regional, though some achieve wide acclaim. But there is no standardization of common names, and anglers in different regions often refer to the same aquatic insect with different common names. To help further explain, let's look at one famous Eastern mayfly, the Hendrickson.

"Hendrickson" is a common name, given to the mayfly by famous fly tier and state conservation officer, Roy Steenrod, along New York's Beaverkill River. Many anglers also know that the Hendrickson's scientific name is *Ephemerella subvaria*. This name shows the mayfly's genus and species (genus=*Ephemerella*, species=*subvaria*).

When writing aquatic insect names, only the genus and species are in italics. It's also common to see only a capitalized initial (the abbreviation for the genus) followed by a period to denote a specific mayfly species, like *E. subvaria*. The genus is abbreviated because it stands for a wide range of its possible species members. It's the species name that really identifies an insect. The genus name is mostly helpful to identify relationships between similar species. So if you're reading about multiple mayfly members that share the Hendrickson genus then you will see: *Ephemerella* spp. The abbreviation spp. is not capitalized because it stands for the word "species," and mayfly species names are not capitalized. When you see spp. it means that there is more than one relevant species; sp. means just a single species.

A small group of mayflies have two species names. The Little Sulphur, common in the eastern United States, (*Ephemerella dorothea dorothea*) and PMD, common in the West, (*Ephemerella dorothea infrequens*) are both examples of this. The double species name looks like a typo, but it's not. It is called a trinomial. These mayflies and any others you see with two species names are considered sub-species. This means that Little Sulphurs and PMDs are closely related, much closer than other mayflies in the *Ephemerella* genus. Think of it this way: if Little Sulphurs (*E. dorothea dorothea*) and Hendricksons (*E. subvaria*) are cousins because they're both in the *Ephemerella* genus, then Little Sulphurs (*E. dorothea dorothea*) and PMDs (*Ephemerella dorothea infrequens*) are more akin to siblings.

Each insect, or any living thing, has also been given a much longer scientific name (also known as taxonomic name), going back to a kingdom designation--but this level of identification is seldom used by anglers. Here's the full Hendrickson name traced back to its Kingdom name:

Kingdom: Animalia
Phylum: Arthropoda
Class: Insecta
Order: Ephemeroptera
Family: Ephemerellidae
Genus: *Ephemerella*
Species: *subvaria*

These classifications can be taken even further with the additions of suborders and superfamilies for those species that have them and even "tribes" for caddisflies. But this detail level provides little help to the fly angler. For angling purposes, it is a good idea to know at least the genus and species names for our most common mayflies, just so we can talk to each other without relying on the often faulty common names. It's important to remember that when using only common names, anglers outside your region and sometime just outside your watershed, won't know to what you are referring. Anglers often times use different names for the same insect. For example: A "Shad Fly" in central Pennsylvania is a Green Drake mayfly (*E. guttulata*), while a "Shad Fly" in New York's Catskill region in an Apple Caddis (*B. appalachia*). This can lead to a great deal of confusion without using a standardized naming system, and, for better or worse, that system is found in Latin, not common, names. And by the way, most aquatic insect names aren't really "Latin." It's probably more correct to say that they've been given Latinized names: names that look and sound like Latin, but have no counterparts in the actual Latin language.

Aquatic entomology is constantly evolving. New research, including DNA testing, is revealing previously unknown relationships between mayfly genera (genera is the plural of genus). When a new insight or relationship is discovered, the insect's name can change in a couple of ways for different reasons.

First, the bug could be placed into a new genus. That's what happened a few years ago when the small yellowish mayfly known as *Heptagenia hebe* was renamed as *Leucrocuta hebe*. The second most common name change has been happening a lot in the last 20 years. A Purdue University entomologist named Patrick Maccafferty has made a large number of discoveries, advancing our understanding of some mayfly genera and their relationships to each other. Many of these mayflies are now named after Maccafferty. For example, the March Brown used to be known as *Stenonema vicarium*, but due to Maccafferty's research it is now known as *Maccaffertium vicarium*.

3

MAYFLIES (EPHEMEROPTERA)

Nymph

Dun

Spinner

Mayfly **nymphs**, such as this *E. guttulata*, breathe through their gills. They spend anywhere from a few months to a couple years living subsurface. Because mayfly nymphs live beside the trout, beneath the water's surface, they are the most commonly eaten mayfly life stage. Mayfly **duns** (*E. guttulata*, above) breathe air after they emerge from their nymphal skin in one of four places: On the river bottom, in the water, on or near the water's surface, and on streamside rocks or vegetation. Mayfly duns and spinners often instigate what many angler believe to be the most fun part of fly fishing—dry fly fishing. Mayfly **spinners** (*E. guttulata*, above) are the final mayfly life stage. They can accumulate around a waterway over several days, their numbers growing with each day, and create fantastic fishing as they mate, lay eggs, and fall spent to the water. This is the mayfly's most vulnerable life stage, and trout often gorge on the dead and dying spinners.

I f matching aquatic insects with artificial flies is the heart of fly fishing for trout, then mayflies are the soul. When most people imagine insects hatching from trout water, they picture these elegant and often dainty creatures.

Mayflies come in a dazzling array of sizes and colors. In North America, there are 23 mayfly families that include 106 genera. All mayflies have six legs and either two or three tails. If you find one with one (or no) tail or fewer legs, then the tails or legs have fallen off the body. This is more common than you may realize.

Fly fishermen have divided mayfly nymphs into four families—clingers, crawlers, burrowers, and swimmers—grouping the insects by where and how they live in their larval or nymph form. Entomologists divide mayflies into families that contain multiple, related genera. The genera are further divided into species, and it's the genera and species names, as well as common names given by fishermen, that nearly all anglers associate with mayflies. For example: *Ephemerella subvaria*—the Hendrickson, or *Ephemera guttulata*—the Eastern Green Drake. Most anglers are not familiar with mayfly family names because they are seldom used, but there is value in understanding the shared traits of mayflies within the same family and group.

Swimming nymphs (*I. bicolor*, above) are able to move through the water like little fish. It's sometimes effective to fish these nymphs with short strips of the fly line, imitating their swimming motion. Use slightly heavier tippets to prevent break-offs because trout strikes can be vicious as they attempt to grab these types of nymphs.

Crawling nymphs (*E. subvaria*, above) amble along the stream bottom's cobbles. These nymphs are best imitated by fishing fly patterns slowly along the streambed (also called dead-drifting). Your flies should occasionally be snagging the bottom if you are properly imitating crawling nymphs.

Fly fishermen have also adopted the terms nymph, dun, and spinner for describing mayfly life stages. But professional entomologists do not use these terms. Instead, they refer to mayfly life stages as larva, subimago, and imago.

Mayflies begin their lives as fertilized eggs. Some species take as long as two years to develop from egg to adult while others take only a couple months. Most mayflies produce one generation per year. That means their hatch consists of cycles with one egg, dun, and mated spinner. But some species produce multiple generations (also called broods).

Mayflies complete an amazing life cycle that begins with gilled creatures that swim, crawl, burrow, or cling beneath the water and ends with air-breathing winged insects that can fly. The mayfly life cycle is considered incomplete because it does not include a pupal, or resting, stage. The process begins as they leave their nymphal skin, also known as a shuck, and become what anglers call emergers--mayflies that are trying to, or just reaching, the water's surface in their progression from nymph to dun. They have all the necessary parts to be called a dun, but at this time, they have not yet attained flight. Most of our important mayfly species emerge in the water and ride along the surface making them excellent targets for trout.

Once mayflies are fully out of the water, either floating on top of it, flying, or resting streamside, they are called duns (subimagos). Most mayfly hatches commence with predominately male members that usually have much larger eyes than females and a clasper beneath their tails. Mayfly duns usually have four wings that stand upright when the insects are at rest. Two of their wings are large and prominent. The other two wings, called hind wings, are usually small, approximately half the size or smaller than

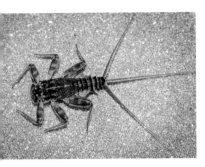 

Clinging nymphs' (*M. vicarium*, above) bodies are flat and aerodynamic so that the water's current doesn't pull them from their rocky perches. Though clingers are most often found holding steadfast to their rocky homes, they sometimes lose hold, either accidentally or intentionally, and drift in the current. They too should be imitated by dead-drifting nymphs near the stream bottom.

Burrowing nymphs (*H. atrocaudata*, above) have well-defined gills along their abdomens and legs especially designed for digging into the substrate. Most of the largest mayflies in North America are burrowers—nearly all of the species we commonly call "Drakes" and "Hex." Burrowing nymphs are best imitated right before and during an emergence. Other than at these times, the nymphs are usually safely tucked into their burrows.

the two main wings. Some mayflies, such as those found in the *Acentrella* species of Blue Winged Olives (also called by the older genus name Pseudos by anglers) only have two wings that lack hind wings, but they are the exception rather than the rule. Mayfly duns usually have opaque wings, sometimes with prominent lines running through them. These lines are called venations.

Most duns take cover in nearby vegetation after emerging, trying to avoid predators like birds, while they rest and prepare to transform into sexually mature spinners (imagos). The time they spend resting as their bodies change is species dependent. Some mayflies change in minutes; others take days. Mayflies do not have functioning mouth parts beyond their nymphal (larva) stage, so they are unable to eat or drink as duns and spinners. Because of this, the mayflies that take the longest to change are often large insects. Their big bodies carry enough nutrients to allow them to survive longer.

Physical traits are often magnified in the spinner stage. Body colors become more intense or change completely, often to shades of orange or red. Tails lengthen and wings usually, but not always, become clear, like translucent cellophane. But some species maintain the prominent venations from their dun wings.

A few mayflies end their transformation in the dun stage and never transform into spinners, but this is rare. Female White Flies (*Ephoron* spp.) do not change into spinners. They are ready and able to mate as soon as they emerge and attain flight. Strangely, male White Flies do become spinners, completing their part of the cycle in a more traditional manner.

At the appropriate time of day, spinners will leave their hiding places to gather over

Most mayflies transform from nymphs into duns while they are still in the water. This gives trout ample opportunities to eat them. Anglers use flush-floating fly patterns called emergers to imitate them.

riffles and mate. The time of day depends on the mayfly species and the time of year in which it lives, but it is most often driven by air temperature and weather. When it's hot, some mate and lay their eggs early in the morning or well after dark. Others wait until just before sunset. Some will complete their cycle throughout the day, though this is usually during cold springtime emergences or in cold tailwaters.

Males are usually the first spinners to begin hovering above the water, looking for mates. They are then joined by females. The insects mate, and then the males die, falling to the water most often with their wings outstretched, largely motionless, in a posture that anglers call "spent." Species that create the best fly fishing opportunities have males that die over the water. But in some species, like the *Paraleptophlebia* spp. (Summer Blue Quills) males fly from the water after mating, never giving the trout an opportunity to eat their spent bodies. And males don't always die immediately after mating once. They are capable of mating with more than one female.

Females allow their eggs to ripen after mating. The timing for this is also species dependent though it generally happens quickly, within minutes. Females then fly upstream and lay their eggs. Some will fly above the water and drop their eggs. Some will dip their abdomens into the water to get the eggs to release, and others will fly close to the water and crawl to the stream bottom to lay their eggs. Some females will fly away from the stream after egg laying, but most will fall spent to the water, providing fish with an easy meal.

IMITATING THE MAYFLY LIFE CYCLE WITH FLIES

Most anglers fish mayfly nymph patterns beneath a strike indicator, often with some kind of weight to make them sink. This weight can either be attached to the leader as split shot or incorporated into flies when they are tied. Indicators are usually attached to a leader at a distance approximately one and one half to two times the depth of the water. Lead weights like split shot are usually attached to the leader 6 to 10 inches above the fly (the first fly if more than one is used).

Most of the time, nymphs should be fished near the stream bottom. You'll know that your flies are in the right zone if they are occasionally ticking rocks and other bottom structure and once in a while you're getting stuck. You should expect to lose some flies if you are fishing correctly. But if you're getting stuck every cast, you're probably using too much weight. Remove some, and try again.

Imitating mayfly emergers is generally accomplished with flush-floating dry flies (*see CDC, Deer Hair, and Snow Shoe emerger section in chapter 7*) that sit partially submerged on the water's surface and partially floating above it to give the illusion of an insect that is leaving its nymphal body. But some mayfly genera like *Epeorus* hatch on the stream bottom and swim to the surface as fully formed duns. These insects are best imitated by swinging wet flies.

You swing wet flies by casting them upstream and then flipping the portion of the fly line between your rod tip and leader upstream (mending) to help them sink. Mending creates slack that helps combat drag on the fly, allowing it to float more naturally or sink more quickly. In fast water, it could be necessary to mend again. After the fly sinks to the bottom and drifts downstream from you, allow the current to grab your fly line and pull it, dragging the fly from the stream bottom toward the surface. This gives the illusion of an insect swimming to the surface to emerge.

Mayfly duns and spinners are usually best imitated by patterns that ride on the water's surface, gliding down the currents drag-free. "Drag-free" means that the flies are floating naturally, without any obvious effect from being tied to your leader and fly line. Drop a leaf onto the water and watch the way it floats downstream, unencumbered and without side-to-side motion. That is floating drag-free, and it is how trout expect mayflies to float after hatching. If your artificial pattern floats unnaturally, it will often be refused because trout are able to tell that something isn't quite right. This is especially true in famous trout fisheries where the fish see a lot of flies and most have been caught before, making them more cautious.

Even small mayflies like Tricos can inspire trout to rise when thousands of them fall to the water after mating. These tiny western Tricos are covered in dew droplets as they wait to transform into spinners at sunrise.

4

CADDISFLIES (TRICHOPTERA)

Larva

Pupa

Adult

Larva, pupa, and adult Tan Caddis (*Hydropsyche* sp.). Wormlike caddis **larvae** breathe through gills and live on the river bottom. **Pupae** transform from larvae to adults. Mayflies and stoneflies do not go through this stage. **Adults** look similar to moths. They come in many sizes and colors and are the most prolific aquatic insect in many rivers and streams. Many adult caddisflies are similar shaped and behave in the same manner. This makes it easy to imitate most caddis adults just by changing the size and color of your fly patterns to imitate the naturals.

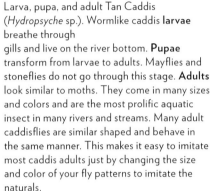

C addisflies are perhaps the most underappreciated aquatic insect family. To many non-anglers, they look like little moths. Adults have wings shaped like a tent, segmented bodies without tails, and antennae that give a moth-like appearance. But unlike moths, caddisflies spend most of their lives living in the water as larvae, which look like little worms. Most, but not all, caddisfly larvae live in some type of case that they build from rocks, sand, plant material, or even their own silk.

Whereas mayflies have an abundance of fly fishing literature dedicated to their existence, there is much less information about caddisflies. Caddis are difficult and confusing to understand because there are so many species that look similar and because one type of caddis that doesn't even exist in your favorite local trout water may be extremely important in a nearby stream. The 20 caddisfly families in North America contain over 1,400 species, and new species are being discovered all the time. Fortunately for anglers, most species have similar behavioral characteristics and techniques for imitating one species can often be used for another.

In *Caddisflies* (the first significant American fly fishing work entirely about caddisflies published in 1981) Gary LaFontaine divided caddisflies into five families according to the cases in which they live: tube-case makers, net spinners, free-living, purse-case makers, and saddle-case makers. But Thomas Ames, in *Caddisflies*,

Fixed-retreat maker caddisflies (*Hydropsyche* spp.) freely wander the stream bottom outside of a case but create nets that look like spider webs. You can often see the nets in shallow areas along the streambed or underneath rocks. Tan Caddis or the Spotted Sedge, members of the *Hydropsyche* and *Symphitopsyche* genera, are probably the most important members of the fixed-retreat makers.

(Stackpole 2009) divides caddis into three families: primitive, fixed-retreat makers, and tube-case makers. I like Ames' approach because it simplifies things a bit. Instead of identifying and separating each caddisfly by the exact type of case, Ames takes a more general approach, organizing them into three groups: those that do not live inside a case (primitive, free-living), those that have a home they live near (fixed-retreat makers, net spinners), and those that construct a case in which they live (tube-case makers, purse-case makers, saddle-case makers).

Unlike mayflies and stoneflies, caddisflies have a complete life cycle with larval, pupal (also called a resting stage), and adult life stages. Caddisflies begin life as eggs that have been deposited in or near the water. Most often female caddisflies do this by flying above the water and releasing their eggs onto the surface. The eggs sink and quickly attach to rocks or other structure. But some species crawl beneath the water to lay their eggs. Some less common species deposit their eggs on dry land, near water, where the larvae can easily crawl into the current after hatching.

It takes the eggs anywhere from a few weeks to a few months to hatch. Some species even over-winter as eggs. After hatching, the larvae usually undergo five instars as they develop (some have more), with the fifth instar taking the longest to complete. An instar occurs as the insect grows and sheds its skin. All mayflies, stoneflies, and caddisflies have instars. The larvae of most species will then live for one year, though some species live for two.

Left: Primitive caddis larvae (*Rhyacophila* sp.) do not build cases or nets. They freely wander among streambed rocks much like mayfly and stonefly nymphs. *Right:* Tube-case makers (*Brachycentrus* sp.) live in trout streams across the country and build shelters from bits of rock or plant material that look like little oil derricks or ice cream cones. These brown conical shaped tubes come in many shapes and sizes depending upon the caddis species and the materials present in the streams in which they live.

At approximately the same time each year, the larvae begin to pupate. This means that they will encase themselves in a cocoon, just like a butterfly or moth, as they transform into winged adults. Those caddis larvae that live in cases simply close the open end of the case before pupating. Others, like members of the free-living *Rhyacophila* genus, create a pupal case from their own silk. The length of the pupation varies with species but most will take two to five weeks, though some species take much longer, even over-wintering for two to three months, as pupa.

After their transformation is complete, the caddis chew their way out of their pupal case and swim to the surface as fully formed, sexually mature adults. Most adults can live for as long as a few weeks (some can survive significantly longer) as they complete their life cycle. Caddis adults can live longer than most mayfly duns because they are able to drink and do not die from dehydration like so many mayflies.

Caddisfly eggs sink to the stream bottom once they are dropped by females. These sticky eggs masses cling to all types of subsurface objects from rocks to sticks and vegetation. During intense egg-laying such as the events that occur during caddis super-hatches like the Mother's Day Caddis, millions of eggs will cover the stream bottom. Trout have been known to eat these eggs.

Unlike mayflies, which mate while they fly, caddisflies remain stationary as they mate, often on streamside vegetation. Males fly away from the water after mating, providing the trout no opportunities to eat them. But females often end their lives in the water after depositing their eggs, creating great fishing opportunities as trout rise to eat them.

Caddisflies mate on dry ground or streamside vegetation, beyond the reach of hungry trout. This ensures that males are seldom available to fish after mating because they usually fly from the water before dying. However, females will be available to trout. Depositing their eggs saps what little energy reserves they have left and leaves them floating helplessly on the water. Anglers call these females "spent" (just like spent mayfly spinners). They are easy targets for trout and usually inspire excellent dry-fly fishing.

IMITATING THE CADDIS LIFE CYCLE WITH FLIES

Caddisflies are vulnerable to trout through much of their life cycle, giving anglers several opportunities for imitating them to catch fish. The first is the larval stage. Caddis larvae become trout food when they drift naturally in the current after becoming dislodged from the stream bottom. These larvae are best imitated by dead drifting fly patterns along the streambed beneath a strike indicator or below a dry fly that is used as a strike indicator.

Caddis pupa imitations are effective for imitating the flies as they near their emergence into adults. Gary LaFontaine broke ground with his Sparkle Pupa patterns for imitating this caddis life stage, and his patterns remain popular today. These flies can be fished with or without intentional movement, though I usually prefer to fish them with a tight line and no indicator.

Tight lining (also called high-stick nymphing) employs a short amount of line outside the rod tip, often only the leader, with the rod held outstretched, slightly leading the flies through deep runs and areas of current, feeling for strikes. When caddis pupae leave their cases and swim to the surface, it's an excellent time to swing wet flies. I use the exact same techniques that were explained in the mayfly section for swinging wet flies.

When emerging caddisflies reach the surface, dry fly imitations are often the best choice. My initial caddisfly adult presentations are usually made without intentional drag. But caddisflies tend to twitch, hop, and jump on the surface as they try to fly, and trout sometimes key on this movement. Anglers often skitter caddis dries to imitate this behavior. You "skitter" a caddis dry by intentionally allowing it to drag on the surface ahead of a rising trout. Hackled patterns work best because they are usually the most buoyant.

Dry flies will be effective again once mating has been completed and the spent females lie on the surface. You will nearly always want these floating drag-free. Some tiers add a small dubbing ball, colored to imitate an egg sac, at the end of their fly pattern's abdomen. Fish can selectively key on this, and it is a good idea to have a few of these flies in your box.

5

STONEFLIES (PLECOPTERA)

Stonefly nymphs (*Pteronarcys* sp., above) look fierce, but they are harmless to people. Stoneflies live anywhere from one to three years as nymphs (depending on species) before they transform into adults.

S toneflies are the least elegant of the big three aquatic insect hatches. To use a football analogy, if mayflies are fly fishing's quarterbacks and caddisflies are running backs and receivers, stoneflies would be the offensive linemen. They're often big, bulky bugs that are clumsy fliers, and they look like something from a monster movie. Stoneflies look like they want to bite you, though I can assure you that they won't.

Most stonefly species require clean, cold water to thrive. Some species can be large—the largest insects fly fishermen imitate. These large stoneflies, often called Golden and Giant Stoneflies in the East and Midwest, and Salmonflies and Golden Stoneflies in the West, have a multiple year life cycle; some live for two years from egg to adult and others for three. This makes them available to trout every day, all year. So they are an important food source.

Adults and nymphs have two antennae on their heads and segmented bodies that always have two tails. Stonefly adults have two sets of wings (four in total) that are held as one over their backs when they are at rest. But they lie flat, not tented like the caddisfly's. In the air, a stonefly's four wings form an X pattern that is easy to see when

Stonefly adults (*Pteronarcys* sp., right) are easy to differentiate from caddis adults. Stoneflies keep their wings flat at rest and they make an X pattern in flight. Caddis wings are usually held like a tent at rest and there is no discernable X when they fly.

you're looking for it. Caddisfly wings do not make this X shape when they fly. The four wings pads are also visible and important to imitate in the stonefly nymph stage. Generally, stonefly adults fly poorly, and they will sometimes fall to the water's surface where they struggle and are often eaten by trout.

Stoneflies, like mayflies, have an incomplete life cycle that does not include a pupal stage. They spend one to three years living subsurface as nymphs before emerging as sexually mature adults. Most, but not all, stoneflies crawl onto exposed rocks or streamside vegetation to complete their metamorphosis; however, some emerge in the water, particularly species that usually hatch in high water conditions most often found in the early spring.

Stoneflies mate on the ground like caddisflies. After mating, the males usually become unimportant for fly fishing because they simply crawl away and die. Often times, females are also unavailable to trout. Some dip their eggs into the water while standing near the shore, never actually getting into the water, and then they too crawl away and die. Others deposit their eggs while flying, dipping and crashing into the water as they try to release their sticky egg mass, leaving the females struggling on the surface after their eggs have gone.

These females become easy meals for trout and sometimes elicit violent strikes and explosive fishing. Strangely, on more than one occasion I have witnessed some stonefly females from the same species depositing their eggs both ways: some are flying and dipping their eggs on the surface while others are releasing them along the shore. After the eggs reach the stream bottom, they hatch, and the nymphs freely wander along the substrate just like mayfly nymphs.

IMITATING THE STONEFLY LIFE CYCLE WITH FLIES

Subsurface stonefly patterns are favorites of dedicated nymph fishermen for one important reason: stoneflies often have a multi-year life cycle, and their nymphs are available year-round, so trout are accustomed to feeding on them. However, the patterns are not always effective. I have found the best time to fish stonefly nymphs to be during high water events in small- to mid-sized streams. They are effective more often in big rivers that naturally maintain a higher water volume. Many stonefly nymphs are large patterns that are easily discerned as fakes in low, clear water. And because the flies are often heavily fortified with lead wraps and beads, they sink quickly. This is good for fast-moving water or deep braids in large rivers, but they often snag too easily in slower or shallower waters.

I usually fish stonefly nymphs in tandem with smaller flies, using the heavy stonefly nymphs to pull the smaller fly deeper into the water column. This gives trout an option of a large obvious meal or one more subtle. I usually choose 3X tippet for attaching the stonefly nymph to my leader with 6 to 12 inches of smaller diameter tippet (usually one to two sizes smaller) for attaching the dropper fly to the stonefly nymph's hook bend. Fairly big strike indicators, like medium to large Thingamabobbers, are a good choice to keep the heavy stonefly nymphs from constantly tangling on the stream bottom. But the nymphs should be fished at the same speed as the current, close to the bottom, to imitate stoneflies that are crawling among the rocks or that have been dislodged and are trying to regain the bottom.

Stonefly dries are not as popular in the East as they are in the West, but many Eastern trout are still caught on these flies each year. In the West, large foam dry flies are often used. The Salmonfly and Golden Stonefly hatches are some of the best and most anticipated of the season, drawing anglers from around the world. Even smaller stoneflies, like the Yellow Sally, can produce epic fishing conditions, but in the East, this is much less common.

Some Eastern fisheries do maintain heavy stonefly populations like the Upper Delaware River's prolific Golden Stones and to a lesser extent, Giant Stoneflies. But anglers can find acceptable stonefly dry fishing even in smaller rivers and streams. Springtime in these waters is an excellent time to fish a tandem with a lead stonefly dry, like a Stimulator, and a smaller nymph like a Beadhead Pheasant Tail for the second, or trailing, fly. It's a good idea to use heavier tippets, seldom lighter than 4X.

Stoneflies often crawl onto streamside rocks or vegetation to transform from nymphs to adults. This one used a streamside tree. It's common to find stonefly nymph shucks by the hundreds on the concrete bridge footings over trout streams.

6

HATCH PROGRESSION AND IMPORTANCE CHARTS

———

The hatch chart is one of the most recognizable features of most fly fishing books and articles. We fly fishers tend to be sticklers for ordered thinking, so the desire to place the timing of aquatic insect hatches into tight little boxes has been passed down for generations. But I'm about to commit heresy here: Most hatch charts are fantasy. There are just too many variables for a static hatch chart to encompass. Stream geography including elevation, water levels, weather, manmade impoundments, and even a touch of the mysterious unknown all collaborate to ensure that mankind's best hatch chart will be little more than an inaccurate guess.

It's impossible to tell you exactly what aquatic insects will be most important on your home water without spending time in that river or stream. And unless you live near an absolutely pristine waterway, chances are that not every hatch listed in my charts will be important for your fishing. You could also find small, localized hatches that are important to you that are not included in these charts. In other words, the charts are a starting point. They show you what's possible, but it's up to each individual angler to determine what's most important for their water.

But hatch charts can do one thing well; they can illustrate hatch progression. Though the myriad of conditions previously mentioned will greatly impact hatch timing, hatch progression in a specific waterway is nearly always the same. Generally, one hatch will follow the next in a specific and ordered way. Hatch chart progressions put the onus on you. You need to visit the water as often as you can to see what's hatching. Then you will know what should follow. I say "should follow" because there is one caveat to all of this: every stream doesn't have every hatch.

In the West, the giant stonefly called a Salmonfly (*P. californica*) will hatch before Tricos begin their emergence. I can't tell you with certainty when the giant stones will begin hatching, but I can assure you that you won't see a Trico in a watershed that has both insects until long after the giant stones have ended. It's the same in the East. I don't know when the Hendrickson hatch will begin, but I do know that if you fish a stream that has both hatches, you will see Hendricksons before Sulphurs.

Some charts list hatches separately for mayflies, caddisflies, and stoneflies. But I find that misleading. Throughout the season, hatches will mix. Some will be waxing while others are waning. It's also quite common for individual trout to feed with their own agenda. So while you might find one fish eating Hendrickson mayflies, the next fish beside it might be selectively feeding on Grannom caddis. This is particularly true with wild fish.

Hatches will overlap and sometimes a couple individual specimens will even appear out of order. But the progression in the charts below show the normal order when the bulk of each hatch appears, taking its place as the most important for its duration.

The following charts rank the most common aquatic insect hatches on a 1 to 5 scale for each of their life stages. A score of 5 means that trout reaction and fishing opportunities are excellent. A 1 score means that the stage is often of little to no importance to fly fishers.

These rankings are highly subjective and are meant to provide only baseline information. Aquatic insect populations and their densities can vary widely from stream to stream and region to region. The importance of an entire hatch, or even a hatch stage, will also vary from stream to stream. Stream characteristics, like thick weed beds that can make nymphing difficult or impossible, will also determine how important some stages are from one stream to the next.

I have tried to combine a lot of factors into the charts. When I'm comparing two spinnerfalls, one that occurs largely during the day and one that occurs well after dark, I have given a higher rating to the daytime spinnerfall. So even though the two hatches are equally heavy and equally received by trout, I have given a higher rating to the hatch that gives anglers the best opportunity to fish it. Hatch distribution is also a factor. A hatch that is found in fewer rivers and streams, like the Winter Caddis (*Dolophilodes distinctus*) in the eastern United States, receives a lower rating than a hatch that is found in nearly every trout stream, like Tan Caddis (*Hydropsyche* and *Symphitopsyche* spp.).

The following chart lists major North American mayfly families with fly fishing significance. Each family member's genus is given an importance ranking. A 1 ranking is for little to no angling importance. This is given because either the mayflies do not exist in that region, or their populations are so small that they are not significant. A 5 ranking denotes great importance because the genus has several important species, or at least one very important species, or a wide geographical range. Where there are two rankings in a column, divided by a dash, it is because an insect is more important in either the East or Midwest. The first number is for the Eastern ranking, the second is for the Midwest.

It's important to understand that within each mayfly family there are multiple genera and species members. Some are important to fly fishers and others are not. I have not listed them all, just those that are commonly found in trout waters. It's interesting to note that some mayfly families important in the western United States are unimportant in the eastern United States and vice versa. Blank "Mayfly Family" column boxes indicate that the insect belongs to the last family named above it.

Eastern and Midwestern Hatches – Importance by Stage

Common Name	Latin Name	Nymph	Emerger/ Dun/Adult	Spinner/ Egg Layer
Winter Stonefly	*Allocapnia* spp.	2	1	1
Winter Caddis	*Dolophilodes distinctus*	3	2	1
Little Black Stonefly	*Taeniopteryx nivalis*	3	3	2
Little Blue Winged Olive	*Baetis* spp.	4	5	5
Early Brown Stonefly	*Strophopteryx fasciata*	2	1	2
Blue Quill	*Paraleptophlebia* spp.	4	4	3
Little Black Caddis	*Chimarra* spp.	4	4	3
Quill Gordon	*Epeorus pleuralis*	1	3	2
Hendrickson	*Ephemerella subvaria*	5	5	5
Black Quill	*Leptophlebia cupida*	2	2	2
Grannom	*Brachycentrus* spp.	5	5	5
Apple Caddis	*Brachycentrus appalachia*	4	4	4
Big Sulphur	*Ephemerella invaria*	5	5	5
Tan Caddis	*Hydropsyche* and *Symphitopsyche* spp.	5	5	5
Golden Stoneflies	*Acroneuria, Agnetina,* and *Paragnetina* spp.	4	3	3
March Brown	*Maccaffertium vicarium*	4	5	3
Little Sister Sedge	*Cheumatopsyche* spp.	2	3	3
Little Sulphur	*Ephemerella dorothea dorothea*	4	5	5
Green Drake	*Ephemera guttulata*	4	5	5
Dark Blue Sedge	*Psilotreta* spp.	2	3	3

Eastern and Midwestern Hatches *continued*

Common Name	Latin Name	Nymph	Emerger/ Dun/Adult	Spinner/ Egg Layer
Giant Stonefly	*Pteronarcys* spp.	3	2	1
Michigan Caddis*	*Hexagenia limbata*	3	5	5
Slate Drake	*Isonychia* spp.	5	5	4
Brown Drake	*Ephemera simulans*	3	5	5
Blue Winged Olive	*Drunella cornuta* and *D. cornutella*	4	5	5
Green Caddis	*Rhyacophila* spp.	5	5	4
Roachlike Stonefly	*Peltoperla* and *Tallaperla* spp.	2	2	1
Callibaetis	*Callibaetis* spp.	1	2	2
Gray Drake	*Siphlonurus* spp.	2	2	3
Light Cahill	*Stenacron interpunctatum*	2	4	4
Cream and Dark Cahills	*Maccaffertium, Stenonema,* and *Heptagenia* spp.	2	4	4
Yellow Drake	*Ephemera varia*	2	3	3
Pink Cahill	*Epeorus vitreus*	2	4	3
Yellow Sally	*Isoperla* spp.	1	3	2
Green Sally	*Alloperla* spp.	1	2	2
Summer Blue Quill	*Paraleptophlebia* spp.	2	3	1
Golden Drake	*Anthopotamus* spp.	1	3	2
Trico	*Tricorythodes* spp.	2	4	5
Summer Hex	*Hexagenia rigida*	1	2	1
Hebe	*Leucrocuta hebe*	2	3	2

Common Name	Latin Name	Nymph	Emerger/ Dun/Adult	Spinner/ Egg Layer
White Fly**	*Ephoron* spp.	2	4	4
Big Slate Drake	*Hexagenia atrocaudata*	1	2	3
Slate Drake (second brood)	*Isonychia* spp.	4	5	3
October Caddis	*Pycnopsyche* spp.	2	3	2
Little Blue Winged Olive (second generation)	*Baetis* spp.	5	5	3

* This hatch occurs in isolated pockets, particularly around the Great Lakes Region. But where it does occur, it is often important.

** Often found in waters too warm for trout. But can be important when it emerges in trout water.

Make sure to look for spider webs near bridges and around street lights. They will often tell you what has been hatching. But remember, it takes aquatic insect bodies a while to completely deteriorate so you may be looking at the vestiges of a hatch that ended three days ago.

Western Hatches – Importance by Stage

Common Name	Scientific Name	Nymph	Emerger/ Dun/Adult	Spinner/ Egg Layer
Little Brown Stone	*Capnia* spp.	1	2	2
Blue Winged Olive	*Baetis* spp.	1	5	5
Western March Brown	*Rhithrogena* spp.	4	4	2
Skwala	*Skwala americana*	3	2	3
Brown Dun	*Ameletus* spp.	1	3	1
Mother's Day Caddis	*Brachycentrus* spp.	4	5	5
Salmonfly	*Pteronarcys californica*	5	5	4
Golden Stone	*Calineuria, Hesperoperla, Doroneuria,* and *Claassenia* spp.	5	5	4
Pale Morning Dun (PMD)	*Ephemerella* spp.	5	5	5
Brown Drake	*Ephemera simulans*	4	5	4
Black Quill	*Leptophlebia* spp.	1	2	1
Lead-Wing	*Isonychia* spp.	2	2	4
Yellow Sally	*Isoperla* and *Alloperla* spp.	5	4	5
Spotted Sedge	*Hydropsyche* spp.	5	5	5
Little Sister Sedge	*Cheumatopsyche* spp.	3	4	4
Hex	*Hexagenia limbata*	4	5	5
Callibaetis	*Callibaetis spp.*	5	4	4
Green Sedge	*Rhyacophila* spp.	2	3	4
Glossosoma	*Glossosoma* spp.	5	4	4

Common Name	Scientific Name	Nymph	Emerger/ Dun/Adult	Spinner/ Egg Layer
Gray Drake	*Siphlonurus* spp.	3	2	4
Pink Albert	*Epeorus* spp.	4	3	3
Flav	*Drunella flavilinea*	4	4	3
Western Green Drake	*Drunella* spp.	5	5	4
Pale Evening Dun (PED)	*Heptagenia* spp.	2	5	4
Trico	*Tricorythodes* spp.	2	4	5
Mahogany Dun	*Paraleptophlebia* spp.	2	4	3
Red Quill	*Timpanoga hecuba*	3	3	3
October Caddis	*Dicosmoecus* spp.	4	3	3

It can be sometimes be difficult to tell the difference between mayflies with a quick glance. This western Ameletus dun looks very similar to a Western March Brown and they can be found hatching at the same time of year.

Important Mayfly Families and Genera in the East, Midwest, and West

Family	Genus	Common Name EM	Importance EM	Common Name W	Importance W
Ametletidae	Ametletus	None	1	Brown Dun	3
Baetidae	Acentrella	Pseudo	4	BWO	3
	Baetis	Little Blue Winged Olive	5	Little Blue Winged Olive	5
	Callibaetis	Speckle-Wing	1	Speckle-Wing Dun	4
	Centroptilum	None	1	None	1
	Plauditus	None	1	None	1
	Procloeon	None	1	None	1
Baetiscidae	Baetisca	Armored Mayfly	2	None	1
Caenidae	Caenis	Angler's Curse	2	Angler's Curse	1
Ephemerellidae	Attenella	Small Blue Winged Olive	2	Small Blue Winged Olive	2
	Drunella	BWO, Cornuta	5	Western Green Drake, Flav	5
	Ephemerella	Sulphur, Little Sulphur, Hendrickson	5	Pale Morning Dun	5
	Eurylophella	Chocolate Dun	1	Chocolate Dun	1
	Serratella	Little Olive	2	None	1
	Teloganopsis	Little Black Quill	2	None	1
	Timpanoga	None	1	Red Quill	3

Family	Genus	Common Name EM	Importance EM	Common Name W	Importance W
Ephemeridae	*Ephemera*	Brown Drake, Eastern Green Drake, Yellow Drake	5	Brown Drake	3
	Hexagenia	Hex, Big Slate Drake, Michigan Caddis	3-5	Hex, Michigan Caddis	3
	Litobrancha	Dark Green Drake	2	None	1
Heptageniidae					
	Cinygmula	None	1	Dark Red Quill	2
	Ecdyonurus	None	1	Ginger Quill	2
	Epeorus	Quill Gordon, Big Sulphur, Pink Cahill, Vitreus, Salmon Spinner	4	Pink Lady, Pink Albert	3
	Heptagenia	Cahill	1	Pale Evening Dun	4
	Leucrocuta	Hebe, Little Yellow Quill	2	Pale Evening Dun	2
	Maccaffertium	Cahill, March Brown, Gray Fox, Cream Cahill, Dark Cahill	5	None	1

East, Midwest, and West *continued*

Family	Genus	Common Name EM	Importance EM	Common Name W	Importance W
	Nixe	None	1	None	1
	Rhithrogena	None	1	Western March Brown, Western Red Quill	4
	Stenacron	Light Cahill	3	None	1
	Stenonema	Cream Cahill	2	None	1
Isonychiidae	*Isonychia*	Slate Drake, White Gloved Howdy, Iso	5	Lead-Wing	2
Leptohyphidae	*Tricorythodes*	Trico	5	Trico	5
Leptophlebiidae	*Leptophlebia*	Black Quill, Borcher Drake	3	Western Black Quill	2
	Paraleptophlebia	Blue Quill, Summer Blue Quill, Paralep, Little Mahogany Dun, Jenny Spinner	5	Mahogany Dun	3
Metretopodidae	*Siphloplecton*	None	2	None	1
Polymitarcyidae	*Ephoron*	White Fly	3	White Fly	2
Potamanthidae	*Anthopotamus*	Golden Drake	3	Golden Drake	1
Siphlonuridae	*Siphlonurus*	Gray Drake	2-3	Gray Drake	3

Eastern Hendrickson mayflies hatch when forsythia's yellow flowers are blooming. Pictured here is a female Hendrickson dun resting on a forsythia bush near Central Pennsylvania's Penns Creek.

PHENOLOGY

While no chart can provide certainty as to when a hatch will begin, there is a natural indicator that will tell you. It's called phenology. Phenology studies the relationship between plant and animal life cycles that are based upon climactic and seasonal changes. For fly fishing purposes, phenology looks at the timing of blooming flowers and plants and the aquatic insects that hatch simultaneously.

Once you understand the plants that bloom during the same time as a particular hatch begins, you'll no longer need a hatch chart. For example, in the eastern United States, Hendricksons begin hatching when forsythia has yellow blooming flowers. It doesn't always happen exactly at the same time, but when you see open forsythia flowers, you'll know that Hendricksons are either already hatching or just about to hatch in the next couple of days.

There have been several books written about phenology and other books have mentioned these insights. In *The Phenological Fly*, Bob Scammell looks at the correlation between wildflowers and Western hatches. And the books *Pocketguide to Pennsylvania Hatches* and the *Pocketguide to New York Hatches* both offer phenological correlations for all of the important Eastern hatches. In spite of this, the hatch order in the charts and the importance rankings are still good places to begin if you are trying to anticipate the progression and angler-significance of aquatic insect emergences.

7

SELECTING THE
BEST FLY PATTERN

It's difficult to imitate the wide, flat shape of clinger nymphs with artificial flies, but creating a flattened lead underbody is one way to do it. This *E. vitreus* clinger nymph is camouflaged against the stream bottom where it holds tight against the current by grasping flat rocks.

The depth of your aquatic insect knowledge will be unimportant for catching trout if you do not understand how to translate that knowledge into choosing effective fly patterns and fishing tactics. Part of that translation is understanding the three most vital aspects of aquatic insect imitation: trigger mechanisms, masking hatches, and drag. Master these and your numbers of caught trout will increase exponentially.

TRIGGER MECHANISMS, MASKING HATCHES, AND DRAG

Anglers who wish to tie or purchase the best fish-catching flies need to understand trigger mechanisms. A trigger mechanism is a fly pattern component that makes a fish choose to eat it. Many times a trout has swum beneath my dry fly, looked at it, and refused to eat it. Those flies did not have good trigger mechanisms for that fish on that day.

This is a relatively common phenomenon, particularly in famous fisheries where the trout are often caught and released more than once during a fishing season. These fish have been programmed to be more cautious when they feed, making them difficult to catch. But they are also often the largest fish, so it's hard to just ignore them in favor of easier targets. So how does an angler find a trigger mechanism?

First, you need to make sure that you're imitating the proper aquatic insect hatch. On fertile waters, it's common for more than one insect to be hatching at a time. Wild fish are often individualistic feeders so, simultaneously, one might be eating mayfly spinners while another is feeding on midges and yet one more is eating caddisflies. Anglers call these overlapping insect emergences masking hatches, particularly if one hatch is heavy and obvious while the other hatches are sparser.

Once you determine what the fish is eating, then you need to find the best fly pattern with a triggering mechanism. This can be a large, oversized wing or heavy hackle that gets the fish's attention. Using flies that are tied larger than the naturals during heavy mayfly emergences and spinnerfalls is sometimes a triggering mechanism. Adding a little bit of flashy, synthetic materials to your fly patterns can sometime trigger a trout to feed. Incorporating a trailing shuck that makes the fly look more vulnerable will often work. But just about anything that can be a triggering mechanism can also be the reason a trout won't eat your fly. So how do you know where to start?

There is no easy, one-size-fits-all answer. You might have to try several fly patterns, one at a time, and let the fish tell you what is best. Generally you want to fish as simply as possible. So I start my day with natural colored flies, sized as close to the natural as possible, on the longest leader I can fish for that given water (small streams will require shorter leaders than large rivers), and I fish those flies drag free.

When an artificial fly floats unnaturally because it is tied to the fly rod, it is called drag. Unnatural drag is probably the greatest hindrance for catching fish. This phenomenon is the exact opposite of a triggering mechanism and is more akin to a large neon sign screaming, "Do not eat me!" You can combat drag in two ways: Using longer leaders with finer tippets and by mending the fly line.

You can mend the line by moving it to a place where the effects of drag are least. Aerial mends, like the reach cast, are done in the air before the fly line lands on the water. You perform a reach cast by smoothly sweeping the rod upstream as the line straightens, just before it settles to the water. This cast creates slack in the system by putting the fly downstream of the leader and line. The fly can now float drag free until the line and leader catch up to it. You can also mend on the water by gently flipping the fly line between your rod tip and leader up or down stream to control drag.

If I'm not catching fish and I'm getting good drag-free drifts, then it's time to try something else—perhaps using another fly pattern, or fishing the same pattern differently, or imitating another aquatic insect altogether. The only way to know is to try. And it's this game, seldom played the same way with the same flies two days in a row, that keeps us from getting bored even after fly fishing for decades.

DRY FLIES

For many anglers, the lure of catching a trout on a dry fly was the reason they started fly fishing. Few fly fishing moments are more visually stunning than watching a trout

Burrower mayflies like this *Hexagenia atrocaudata* often struggle to emerge from their nymphal shucks on or near the surface, making parachute dry flies effective imitators.

rising through the water to meet you and your fly at the surface. But how do you know from which of the many patterns out there to choose? There are advantages and disadvantages to each type and understanding them will help you have a better day on the water.

Dry fly styles can look radically different from each other, but there's a reason for that. Water types, weather conditions, and individual species' hatching characteristics can all combine to ensure that a dry fly style that works well for one hatch may not be as effective for another. Or a style that works well in bright sunny weather won't be as good when it's cloudy and rainy. The final, and perhaps most important, reason for the various dry fly styles is that dry flies are used to imitate more than one part of an emergence. You can use dry flies to imitate emergers, cripples, duns, and spinners whereas nymph patterns are only used to imitate aquatic insect larval stages.

The perfect dry fly style, the one that works in every instance, doesn't exist. But most fish aren't perfectly selective either. So much of the time, it really doesn't matter. If you fish high-mountain trout streams where the fish are always hungry and will eat almost any fly, then an exacting imitation is seldom important. If you're a fish counter then it may not matter for you either. I know a few fly fishers like that. While I'm stuck for a half hour working one difficult fish, they freely move up and down the river, looking for the most cooperative targets. There is nothing wrong with that approach if it makes you happy.

But if you're the fly fisher who wants to catch every rising trout you find, including the trout that no one else was able to catch, then understanding the relationship between hatch characteristics and fly pattern styles may help you get closer to that goal. And this is the real purpose of this book. By understanding the strengths and weaknesses of various types of fly patterns and how they are chosen to imitate specific traits found within aquatic insect families, the angler has a complete systematic approach to decode any hatch they may find. To help illustrate what I'm suggesting, let's begin by looking at a fishing scenario that I first described in an article for *Fly Fisherman* magazine.

I found three trout rising within a small pocket in the Delaware River's Lower East Branch. Pink Cahills *(E. vitreus)* were emerging, fluttering from the water and gliding on gentle air currents through the soft light of a falling sun. I tied a size 14 Cahill Compara-dun to my leader and made an accurate cast. The fly landed, drifted a foot, and was gently inhaled by a healthy trout. I released the fish, dried my fly, and cast to the next one. Just like the first trout, a white mouth opened, my fly disappeared, and another big fish was played and brought to my net. When I think back to that day, I'm surprised that I can't remember if those trout were browns or rainbows or exactly how big they were, but I remember everything about the third fish.

I put the same fly over the third fish, and it was ignored. I cast, recast, and kept casting for the next fifteen minutes. But the fish never even glanced at my fly, though it kept occasionally rising. The problem couldn't have been my leader length, tippet size, or lack of a good drift. All three trout had been rising close to each other, and if all of those things were good enough for the first two fish, they should have worked for the third.

I cut the fly from my leader and sat for a few minutes, watching the third fish rise. It wasn't eating every insect that floated over it. This fish was picky. Finally, a Cahill emerged through the film and hopped once on the surface before the third fish ate it. I now knew what to do. I tied on a Catskill-style Cahill and caught that fish on my first cast. It was a plump, thirteen-inch brook trout, the smallest of the three, yet the most difficult to catch.

What made the Catskill fly the right choice? With all the dry fly styles available at your local fly shop—Compara-duns, Catskill styles, Thoraxes, CDC or Snowshoe Emergers, Parachutes, and many others—how do you know which one will work the best?

The key to catching that third fish was the information I knew about the way in which Pink Cahills (*Epeorus* genus mayflies) emerge, and how their emergence can be best imitated with specific dry fly styles. Pink Cahills emerge on the stream bottom and swim to the surface as fully formed duns. Because of this, they are often quickly ready to fly once they reach the water's surface. A Catskill-style fly, resting high on its hackle, looks like a mayfly that is quickly ready to fly away. It was a better imitation for this particular hatch than a Compara-dun that sits deeper in the surface film, appearing more stationary. The first two fish didn't care. They were eating whatever floated past them. But that third fish was more selective. And it took a more scientific approach to fool it. Had I not known the hatching characteristics of *Epeorus* genus mayflies, I may not have caught that fish.

DRY FLY STYLES TO MATCH MAYFLY FAMILIES

You can use specific characteristics of individual aquatic insect hatches to learn how to best imitate any hatch with the most logical fly pattern choice. And if you do, you'll have a great advantage over anglers who are just catching the easy trout or occasionally getting lucky when a more selective fish eats their fly.

To best illustrate my point, let's take a closer look at four different mayflies from four different families that are found throughout North America and represent each of the four mayfly groups: Cahills (*Epeorus* sp., Clingers), Tricos (*Tricorythodes* sp., Crawlers), Brown Drakes (*Ephemerella simulans*, Burrowers), and Little Blue Winged Olives (*Baetis* sp., Swimmers).

I picked these mayflies because members of their genera are important to trout anglers across the country, from Montana to Maine. The methods and fly patterns described for these four mayflies will often produce excellent results when imitating most of their family's members.

CLINGERS: Catskill Style and Epeorus Cahills

The Heptageniidae family of clinger mayflies includes several Cahill genera (*Epeorus, Maccaffertium, Heptagenia, Stenonema, Stenacron,* and *Cinygmula*), Eastern and Western March Browns (*Maccaffertium vicarium* and *Rithrogena morrisoni*), and several other mayfly genera well known to fly fishers. Though some of this family's members are important in the East, and some are important in the West, the *Epeorus* genus is perhaps the most geographically significant across the United States. *Epeorus vitreus,* the Pink Cahill, can be important in the East, and the most important Western *Epeorus* species is probably the Pink Albert, *E. albertae.*

Clinger mayflies usually live in gravelly stretches of

Clinger nymphs are shaped wide and flat, which helps them hold onto rocks in the riffles and glides where they are most often found, like this section of the Lamar River in Yellowstone National Park.

moderate to fast moving water, though some can inhabit more placid currents. Some genera emerge nearer the surface, but others, like several members of the *Epeorus* genus, emerge on the stream bottom and swim to the surface as duns. Because they are already free from their nymphal shucks when they reach the surface, they usually escape to the air quickly. That's why you seldom see Cahill fly patterns tied with trailing shucks. After I saw the brookie eat the Pink Cahill that moved, I knew that a Catskill-style fly would be my best option for imitating that movement, though a Thorax-style fly probably would have worked just as well.

Catskill- and Thorax-style flies stand high on their hackles and tails with their bodies above the water. This posture not only gives the illusion of movement, but subtle breezes make these flies shutter on the water's surface. They can also be purposely skittered to look like insects trying to fly.

It's rare for clingers to appear on the surface with an attached trailing shuck like a burrowing mayfly, though fly patterns that incorporate trailing shucks are known to be effective for some clinger species like Eastern March Browns. But Catskill and Thorax ties are still a good bet even for this hatch because fish are often feeding on the duns in riffles where Catskill and Thorax styles ride high, dry, and visible to anglers.

CRAWLERS: Compara-duns and Tricos

Crawler nymphs are some of the most important and widely distributed in North America. The Ephemerellidae, Leptohyphidae, and Leptophlebiidae families all include crawler genera. Ephemerellidae contains many of our most important mayflies: Hendricksons, Sulphurs, and *cornuta* Blue Winged Olives in the East and Western Green Drakes and PMDs in the West. The Leptophlebiidae family includes Black Quills (*Leptophlebia* sp.) and various *Paraleptophlebia* species, also known as Blue Quills, while the Leptohyphidae family's most prominent member is the Trico.

The Eastern Pink Cahill, *E. vitreus*, emerges on the stream bottom and swims to the surface as a fully formed dun. Although its common name includes the "Cahill" designation, it is not related to any of the other mayfly species anglers call Cahills. Pink Cahills are related to Quill Gordons (*E. pleuralis*), another example of the confusion caused by using common names.

Tricos emerge throughout the United States during the summer months. What they lack in physical size they make up in abundance, falling spent to the water by the thousands during spinner falls.

Crawlers are able to live in varied habitats, so it's common to find them anywhere from the edges of riffles to slow pools. They are a diverse collection of mayflies with some genera sharing clinger, and some swimmer, traits. But most crawlers migrate before emerging, walking from areas of current to slower water where their transformation is more easily achieved. Their transformation methods often leave them riding surface currents for an extended period, sending them sailing down into pools even after emerging from the edges of riffles.

Because crawler duns are often found in pools where fish can easily scrutinize artificial fly patterns, I prefer the Compara-dun's slim profile for imitating most of them, including Tricos. You can tie the flies with or without a trailing shuck to imitate emergers. Male Tricos hatch in the middle of the night, so their emergence won't provide many fishing opportunities. But females hatch in the morning, the exact time depending upon air and water temperatures. The hatching females are sometimes overlooked by anglers waiting for the spinnerfall. A nice flat pool below a riffle is a great place to fish a standard or CDC Compara-dun to trout rising to emerging Trico females. The sparse materials used to tie Compara-duns—dubbing for the body, CDC or deer hair for the wing, and a tailing material—makes it easy to tie these diminutive flies.

BURROWERS: *Parachutes with Trailing Shucks and Brown Drakes*

Burrowing mayflies are some of the most anticipated of the season. They are almost always large insects that sometimes hatch in incredible numbers, elevating their emergences into event status for fly anglers. Burrowers live in small tunnels or depressions that they dig into streambeds. They are highly sensitive to light and most often emerge in the last hour of daylight, early in the morning, or at night, though cloudy days or shaded areas along streams can instigate daytime emergences.

Most burrowers are members of the Ephemeridae family, which includes the Eastern Green (*E. guttulata*), Dark Green (*L. recurvata*), and Yellow (*E. varia*) Drakes as well

Brown Drakes are one of a small handful of mayflies that are the exact same genus and species across North America.

as the *Hexagenia* genera. There are several burrowers in other families that can also be important to anglers, including White Flies (*Ephoron* sp.) in the Polymitarcyidae family and Golden Drakes (*Anthopotamus* sp.), a strange mayfly in the Potamanthidae family that straddles the line between a burrower and a crawler.

Brown Drakes (*E. simulans*) are one of the most important members of the Ephemeridae family because they are found across the country, and it's pretty rare for one mayfly, of the exact genus and species, to be found inhabiting such a vast region.

My preferred dry fly style for fishing Brown Drakes and other Ephemeridae family members during daylight hours is a parachute with a trailing shuck. I make the demarcation between daylight and darkness patterns for members of this family for a couple reasons. Parachutes ride flush in the surface film right where the big drakes and Hexes emerge, and a dark brown Darlon or Antron trailing shuck is an excellent imitator of a big burrowing mayfly's nymph

Blue Winged Olives are perhaps the most common hatch on trout streams across the country. They often appear on gray, rainy days and are readily received by the fish.

case, which often fills with air and floats while the dun is trying to escape it. But Brown Drake and other Ephemeridae emergences often become so intense, and continue well after dark, that the flush riding characteristics of parachutes become a hindrance because they are difficult for anglers to see in low light.

I prefer oversized Wulff- and Catskill-style flies for imitating the big burrowers after dark for the same reason I preferred them for imitating clinger mayflies: They are highly visible and tend to float a long time because their bodies sit above the water.

SWIMMERS: Curved Emergers and Little Blue Winged Olives

As their name implies, swimming mayflies are capable swimmers, flitting about streambeds like little fish. Baetidae is perhaps the most prominent swimming family nationwide for anglers. It includes the *Baetis* and *Acentrella* genera, mayflies anglers call Little Blue Winged Olives, and they provide some of fly fishing's staple hatches.

Olives are famous for appearing on rainy days, often in remarkable numbers, and creating quite a surface feeding frenzy from the fish. *Baetis* often drift in the current while they emerge just beneath the surface, usually occurring during cold weather at the beginning and end of the season. Because of these traits, they have a proclivity for difficult emergences as they struggle to flee their nymphal shuck. This makes CDC and Snowshoe Emergers with trailing shucks, tied on curved, fine wire hooks deadly for imitating them. The way a curved hook curls a brown Darlon or Antron shuck beneath the surface while keeping the wing and some of the body above the water is just an ideal imitation of the natural.

Gray Drakes (Siphlonuridae family, *Siphlonurus* genus) and Slate Drakes (Isonychiidae family, *Isonychia* genus) are swimmers not included in the Baetidae family. Gray Drakes can be locally important in the United States, while Slate Drakes are important in the eastern states. Gray and Slate Drakes are more agile swimmers than *Baetis* and readily glide through riffles while Little Blue Winged Olives generally prefer to spend their lives with short swimming jaunts along weed beds.

I've often read that all *Isonychia* emerge on streamside rocks, out of the water, and that any duns found on the water have either fallen there or been blown by the wind. It is true; many Slate Drakes emerge on streamside rocks. You can see their shucks congregated there every spring and fall, but they emerge in the water too. I've caught most of my *Isonychia*-eating trout with CDC emergers. Contrary to what is often written, Slate Drakes must emerge in-river often enough for trout to key on them. I've found too many of their duns floating on calm, windless days to believe the dry-ground-only emergence myth.

DRY FLY STYLES

As you can see by the previous scenarios, the style of dry flies that you choose should be tailored to the type of mayfly that you are imitating. Next we'll examine the most common styles of dry flies to identify their strengths for imitating specific mayfly, caddisfly, and stonefly traits.

Though this Adams was designed in Michigan, it is tied in the Catskill style, which originated in New York's Catskill Mountains.

MAYFLY DRY FLY STYLES

Catskill Style

Catskill-style dry flies have existed since the early 20th century. Fly fishing historians trace them back to Theodore Gordon who spent most of his life living and fishing in New York's Catskill Mountains. So what is a Catskill-style dry fly?

At its core, a Catskill-style dry is a sparsely tied fly with a quill or dubbed body, wings of wood duck, goose quill, or teal feathers, a tail formed from a clump of the stiffest hackle fibers, and a few wraps of hackle wound perpendicular to the hook shank. Though anglers today still argue over the exact dimensions of a properly tied Catskill fly, in truth, there is no standard, only generalities passed down by great historic tiers like the Dettes, Darbees, and Rube Cross.

Western fly fishers have adapted the Catskill style to meet the needs of the more rough and tumble Western rivers where increased floatation characteristics may be more important than subtlety. They have added extra hackle, thicker wings of synthetic material and calf body hair, and made the dubbed bodies a little thicker to trap more air. And the Catskill fly continues to catch trout across the country and around the world today just as it has done for the last 100 years.

With all of today's modern flies, do you really want to use a style that's over 100 years old? Yes. Here's why: Sparsely tied Catskill flies are good at providing the illusion of movement. When properly tied, these flies stand high, resting on their tails and hackles, which trap air pockets between their fibers. At times, even parts of their body floats above the surface. A gentle breeze can make them shudder, giving the impression of a mayfly that's just about to fly from the water's surface. This makes them ideal for imitating mayfly families that emerge on the stream bottom and leave the water's surface quickly such as many species of clingers. Catskill flies are also a good all-around style. They are not ideal for rough water, though their hackles do help them float well. And they do not give the best flush-floating silhouette, but their material sparseness still makes them useful for fishing flat pools. Catskill flies also excel at dusk and after dark because they sit above the water where they are more visible to anglers than some other styles.

Wulff patterns can be tied in many different colors to imitate many different medium to large mayflies. This Royal Wulff is an attractor pattern—not meant to imitate a specific insect; it just looks buggy.

Wulff Patterns

If you take a Catskill-style fly and bulk it up by adding more material, and wings and tails from calf or deer hair, you have a Wulff-style fly. Wulff-style flies are named for legendary fly fisherman, Lee Wulff. Today Lee Wulff is best remembered through his wife, Joan Wulff, and their famous fly fishing school on the Upper Beaverkill River in New York. The patterns that bear Wulff's name are excellent dry fly choices for fishing in the heaviest rapids to imitate clingers. Their thick materials trap air and make them buoyant, so they're also a good choice for night fishing when it's difficult to know if your fly is still floating.

I also prefer Wulff patterns for imitating the heaviest mayfly hatches and spinnerfalls that occur near and after dark, like those associated with burrowing mayflies such as Drakes and Hexes. Wulff patterns stand out among the crowds of naturals during these mega hatches. They are easier for me to see and their bulkiness also seems to make the trout choose them from among the naturals as a big bite of protein.

The Parachute Adams is an excellent all-around dry fly pattern. It can be tied small to imitate tiny Blue Winged Olive or Blue Quill mayflies or tied larger and used to imitate Gray Drakes. It can also be fished as a searching pattern when nothing is hatching.

Parachute Style

Parachute-style flies evolved from an English fly pattern called the Gyro. Parachutes have hackle wound onto a post so that it lays horizontal to the hook shank. These posts can be made from synthetic materials or various types of hair or feathers. Tails are usually made from hackle fibers or synthetic materials to represent a mayfly's trailing shuck. A trailing shuck imitates the empty skin left as a mayfly changes from a nymph into a dun. Bodies are most often dubbed, though quill or twisted bucktail can also be effective.

Parachutes have several advantages for imitating mayflies. As stated earlier, the addition of a trailing shuck allows anglers to imitate two mayfly stages at once--duns and emergers—and this also makes them an excellent choice for imitating large burrowing mayflies that sometimes have a difficult time escaping their nymphal shucks. Because their hackle lies horizontal to their bodies, parachutes ride flush in the surface film, creating an excellent profile for imitating mayflies in slow, flat water where crawler duns can also be found. Parachutes are not the best choice for heavy, turbulent pocket water or riffles, though they can be used here in a pinch. But because they sit so close to the surface, they will quickly become waterlogged and sink.

A parachute's post or wing is less visible to fish. This allows anglers to use white or even fluorescent colored materials for the post, making parachutes a highly visible option for imitating small, normally hard to see mayflies. Parachutes can also be used as an easy-to-see imitation of spent mayfly spinners because their flush-riding hackle looks similar to outstretched spinner wings.

Compara-dun wings can be tied with deer hair, snowshoe rabbit fibers, synthetic yarns, or CDC feathers. The different materials provide greater or lesser amounts of buoyancy and give the flies a little different look, sometimes important for fooling highly pressured trout.

Compara-duns and Sparkle Duns

Compara-duns were invented by Al Caucci and Bob Nastasi to give a more natural appearance to dry fly imitations. The basic design was inspired by another dry fly pattern, the Haystack, which was popularized throughout New York's Adirondack Mountain region by legendary fly tier Fran Betters. The Sparkle Dun was created by Western fly tier, Craig Mathews. The only difference between Compara-duns and

Sparkle Duns is that the Sparkle Dun adds a trailing shuck, most commonly formed from a synthetic material such as Antron or Darlon, though feather fibers and other materials can also be used. The shuck's addition makes the fly double as a dun and emerger and often increases its effectiveness.

Compara-duns and Sparkle Duns are best used in flat pools or braided water where they are excellent hatch-matching tools. I really like to use this style of fly when imitating crawlers or swimmers: flies that tend to spend a little longer on the water's surface after becoming duns, giving fish ample time to scrutinize them. The sparse materials used to tie the flies—tailing material, dubbed, quill, or twisted bucktail bodies, and deer hair or CDC for the wings makes the patterns popular with anglers and effective for fooling picky fish. But the sparseness also makes the flies a little less buoyant for fishing heavy pocket water or riffles, causing them to sink more readily than Catskill- and Wulff-style patterns.

Flush floating, curved-hook dry flies, like these CDC Burke and Deer Hair March Brown emergers, often catch picky trout that refuse more high floating dry flies.

CDC, Deer Hair, Bucktail Body, and Snow Shoe Emergers

These emerger patterns all share a few common traits. First is a curved hook. Fine wire scud hooks are the most common choice, though these hooks limit the hatches you can imitate. Most hook manufacturers do not produce a fine wire scud model larger than an 8 or 10. Because the hook shank is curved, it makes the bodies look even shorter and it's therefore difficult to imitate large mayflies like drakes or Hexes. But for smaller mayflies, curved-hook emergers are absolutely deadly.

These patterns are simple to tie and most are identical except for the wing material. As their name suggests, CDC, Deer Hair, and Snow Shoe Emergers all have different wing material. These materials just give the fish a varied look and some anglers prefer one or more over the others. I do not have a strong preference, and I generally use all of them interchangeably. Each of these fly styles is commonly tied with a trailing shuck. The flies work best in flat pools, gentle runs, and braided water where their sparseness and position in the water (wings rest above and bodies below) makes them excellent mayfly emerger imitations for all types of swimmer, crawler, and burrowing mayflies.

Bucktail Body Emergers can be tied with any of the aforementioned wing materials though I generally prefer CDC or snow shoe rabbit. Bucktail body flies incorporate various colors of bucktail fibers and thread twisted together to make a rope. The rope is then wrapped along the hook shank to make a quill-like body. The results are a segmented body of mixed colors, just like a real mayfly.

This Last Chance Cripple, created by the famed western fly tier, Rene Harrop, is great for imitating mayflies that are struggling to emerge from the water's surface

Cripples

Flies known as cripples are designed to imitate aquatic insects that are unable to quickly emerge from the water's surface as they hatch. There are several reasons why insects become cripples. They could have been damaged in some way in their nymph or larval state, perhaps during a high water event or a near-miss from a predator. Maybe an angler damaged them by pinning them to rocks when they were crossing a stream. But perhaps the most common reason is weather. Cold temperatures, either from naturally occurring weather or from the unnatural conditions created by tailwater releases, as well as extreme wind can also cause flies to emerge in a compromised state. Crippled flies are often highly targeted by trout that seem to know they are an easy target because they cannot flee. Fish sometimes key on these insects to the exclusion of all others during hatches. And cripples can come from any of the four mayfly types: clingers, crawlers, swimmers, and burrowers. That's why every angler needs a few cripple patterns in their boxes.

Hi-Vis Dry Flies

If you're having trouble seeing your dry on the water you have a couple of options. First, you can move to the opposite side of the river or stream. The angle of the sun causes glare on the water's surface, which you may be able to reduce by putting the sun at your back. Second, you can use a larger, more visible dry fly as a lead fly in a two-fly rig. This way, if a fish takes the smaller dry that's difficult to see, the larger dry will move or sink, just like it would if you're fishing a dry fly and nymph tandem rig. Seeing where the large, visible fly lands on the water can also help you find your smaller less visible fly. Third, you can cast near where you see a fish rise and gently strike at any rises

Hi-vis dry flies incorporate bright materials, often synthetics, into their wings so that anglers can see them better. Caddisflies, stoneflies, and mayflies can all be tied in hi-vis versions.

close where you expect your fly to have landed. This is often the only way to catch fish rising to dry flies after dark. The final way to combat the difficulty of seeing your dry fly is to tie or buy it in a hi-vis version.

Most dry flies used to imitate aquatic insect species can be tied in hi-vis versions, but often it's small mayflies such as Blue Winged Olives or Tricos that are tied this way. Their diminutive size combined with their dull coloration and proclivity for hatching in large numbers can make it very difficult to find your artificial imitation on the water. The hi-vis part of these flies is most often a brightly colored post used in a parachute-style dry fly. This is done because parachutes sit flush in the water, making them already difficult to see and because fish can sometimes be repulsed by bright, unnatural colors used in dry fly construction. But the single, upright post on a Parachute-style fly is much less visible to fish than the wings on other dry fly styles such as Catskill-style or Wulffs.

Other Dry Fly Styles for Mayflies

There are many other dry fly styles, in addition to those previously mentioned, that can be used to catch trout. Some of them, like the Truform flies that I developed, have specific tasks in mind: Truform flies are meant to provide a realistic mayfly posture for large mayflies size 14 and larger.

Conduct some research. Ask some friends. And experiment with patterns like Hackle-wing Duns, Paraloops, Two-feather flies, porcupine quill flies, Truform flies, Bucktail Body flies, and the myriad of other dry fly patterns that are available today. Part of the fun of imitating aquatic insects is learning something and new dry fly patterns are perfect for that. When you are looking at a new style of dry, think of the four mayfly types and how their characteristics can be imitated by the form of the new fly. Perhaps one of these lesser-known styles will fool the largest trout of your life. One did that for me.

Many mayfly species turn rusty red as spinners, but some like PMDs and Sulphurs remain closer to their dun color. Hackle- and Antron-wing dry flies, like the one pictured here, are good imitators of this important phase of the mayfly life cycle.

SPENT SPINNER IMITATIONS

Spinner imitations are most commonly constructed with split tails of hackle or synthetic Microfibetts, a dubbed, quill, or twisted bucktail body, and wings of synthetic polypropylene, Antron, or Darlon, though hackle fibers or even cut feathers are also sometimes used. These patterns ride flush in the surface film and generally do a good job of imitating spent mayflies. Generally, synthetic-winged spinner imitations work well at dusk and into darkness because the white material commonly used remains somewhat visible under low light conditions. It also floats fairly well, particularly if it has been greased or dusted with a floatant. Spinner imitations with hackle wings are more effective for fishing spinnerfalls that occur during daylight hours. The feathers are more translucent and not as bulky, giving a more realistic appearance that can be important during daylight when imitations are more easily discerned by trout.

Elk-Hair

X-Caddis

Elk-Hair and X-Caddis have two primary differences: X-Caddis do not include hackle in their construction, and Elk-Hair Caddis do not have a trailing shuck. X-Caddis are great for imitating emerging flies in slower water, while Elk-Hair Caddis are more buoyant for fishing riffles and heavily braided water.

CADDIS DRY FLY STYLES

Caddis dry fly patterns are not as diverse as patterns for mayflies. Most caddisflies look and behave similarly. Their larvae differ mainly by color and the fact that some live in cases and some do not. The shape and style of the cases also differ. It's the same for the adults. Nearly all caddis have wings that are kept folded over their backs when they are at rest. Their bodies look almost identical with an often hairy, six-legged thorax and a segmented abdomen.

By far, the most popular caddis dry fly pattern is the Elk-Hair Caddis. This dry fly can be used to imitate any caddis by simply changing the color of the body's dubbing and the color of its palmered hackle. The color of the deer or elk hair that is used can also be adapted to match naturals, and you can even add extra elements such as CDC (Cul De Canard) feathers beneath the wing, just to give the flies a little different look. Elk-Hair Caddis patterns work well everywhere fish feed on caddis, but because their hackle and hollow deer hair wings trap air, they are buoyant and a particularly good choice for fishing riffled water.

The X-Caddis is a more sparsely tied version of an Elk-Hair Caddis. The pattern's only addition is a synthetic material, such as Darlon or Antron, for a trailing shuck. X-Caddis also have deer or elk hair wings and dubbed bodies but they omit the Elk-Hair Caddis' hackles. Without the hackle, these flies sit a little deeper in the surface film, making them a little less buoyant for fishing fast water but an excellent choice for fishing glides and slower pools.

Stimulator

Sofa Pillow

Stimulators and Sofa Pillows are excellent stonefly dry imitations. The flies can be tied in varying colors to match the naturals. They float great, making them ideal lead flies in tandem rigs.

STONEFLY DRY FLY STYLES

It has become popular with today's anglers to use big foam dry flies for imitating adult stoneflies on the surface. And these bulky, sometimes elaborate, flies do work, particularly on the expansive, windy Western rivers. But older fly patterns such as Stimulators and Sofa Pillows can also work just as well. These standbys are still popular in the East because they can be tied a little more sparsely for heavily fished waters where bulkiness is not often a positive trait. Stimulators have a deer hair tail and wing, a dubbed body that is palmered with hackle, and a few heavier turns of hackle at their head, just behind the hook eye. Their hollow deer hair combines with a great deal of hackle to trap air bubbles, making the flies buoyant; perfect for fishing heavy pocket water as the lead dry fly in a tandem.

Chubbies are one of the most popular Western dry flies because of their easy construction and great buoyancy. But they can work for Eastern anglers too. The flies come in many colors, from those that match the oranges and yellows of Salmonflies or Golden Stones to attractor patterns like the Purple Chubby.

The Chubby Chernobyl, aka the Chubby, and similarly constructed flies are found in most Western anglers' fly boxes. The Chubby is made from buoyant materials—foam, rubber, and synthetic fibers for its body and wing. Just like Stimulators and Sofa Pillows, Chubbies are an excellent choice to use as the lead or indicator fly when fishing a two fly rig. Most anglers tie a nymph to the bend of the hook so that the Chubby functions as a strike indicator for fish that take the nymph. But often, trout will take the Chubby. Chubbies are most often fished during Golden Stone and Salmonfly hatches in the West, or even as makeshift hopper patterns. Though not as popular in the East, Chubby-style flies can be very effective there as well.

WET FLIES AND NYMPHS

While it's difficult to dismiss the thrill of a trout rising to your dry fly, the single most important truth about trout feeding on aquatic insects is that they do so about 90% of the time subsurface. So if you're not fishing flies that sink—wet flies and nymphs—then your time streamside will often be filled with a whole lot of fishing, but sometimes not a lot of catching. Learning to imitate subsurface aquatic insects is vital to being a complete fisherman. Just like dry flies and emergers, nymphs and wet fly patterns also have particular traits that make them fit some of the four mayfly groups better than others. And savvy anglers will use this to their advantage.

WET FLIES

If dry flies and emergers occupy the water's surface and nymphs lay claim to the stream bottom, then wet flies own everything in between. Long before anglers had perfected a dry fly method or fashioned fly patterns to imitate aquatic insect nymphs, fishermen were using wet flies.

Wet flies are traditionally used to imitate species that emerge on the stream bottom like many mayfly clingers, or at least somewhere below the surface (many crawlers and some swimmers emerge just below the surface film). But they can be used for other purposes. One of my little tricks for fooling selectively rising trout is to dust a wet fly with a powdered floatant like Frog's Fanny to make it float. A wet fly's splayed look gives the impression of a crippled mayfly that isn't able to easily flee the water's surface. Trout often key on that type of captive meal. But most anglers fish wet flies subsurface, on the swing, to imitate emergers.

The phrase "on the swing" means that anglers are casting wet flies, often a cast of wet flies (a cast is three or more flies fished together), across the stream current, mending their fly line to help the flies sink, and then letting the force of the water's current drag the flies from the stream bottom toward the surface to create the impression of an emerging insect. I said insect, not mayfly, because wet flies can imitate both emerging mayflies and caddisflies. Because stoneflies are not often in-water emergers, wet flies are less commonly used for them, though they can be effective and are worth trying when other techniques have failed.

There are two prominent types of wet flies—traditional wets and soft hackles—and though each are tied and look a little different, you can use the same fishing techniques for both of them. But some anglers do find soft hackles to be a little more versatile, greasing them to fish almost like dry flies in the film, as well as swinging them subsurface like traditional wets.

Traditional wet flies and soft hackles can be used to imitate both caddis and mayfly emergers. These older-style flies are not as popular for modern anglers as nymph patterns are, but they remain very effective fish-catching tools and every angler should carry some streamside.

Traditional Wet Flies

Traditional wet flies often have tails of soft, webby feather fibers, though some versions don't have tails. Bodies are usually made from water absorbing dubbings, peacock herl, chenille, or synthetic materials. These flies generally have a hackle collar made from soft, webby feathers such as hen hackle, grouse, or partridge. A hackle collar is created by tying a feather around the head of the fly and capturing it with thread or dubbing so that it sweeps back over the body. Occasionally the collar is omitted in favor of a hackle fiber throat soft feather fibers tied in a clump behind the head so that the tips extend toward the hook point. Traditional wets usually have a single wing, often made from goose quill slips, that is swept back over the body.

Soft Hackles

Soft hackles look similar to traditional wets, except in two key areas. Soft hackles usually have no tail and no wing. They have bodies that are constructed with the same materials as traditional wets, and they always have a collar of hackle. The hackle is the most important part of the soft hackle. It is usually longer than the hackle on a traditional wet so that it pulses in the water. A partridge feather is the most common wing material, though grouse, marabou, and even hen hackles are sometimes used. The hackle is always tied swept back over the body, but when the fly is stripped in the water (retrieving the fly by pulling on the fly line), the hackle bends even deeper over the body. Between strips, the hackle pulses and provides the impression of an aquatic insect struggling toward the surface, because of this motion, I generally prefer soft hackles for imitating clingers whereas I prefer traditional wets for many crawlers and swimmers.

NYMPHS

More United States trout are probably caught on nymph imitations than any other type of fly. There are a couple reasons for that. Trout spend most of their time eating nymphs. Because of this, most anglers learn how to fish nymphs before they attempt dry fly fishing. The necessary techniques to fish nymph imitations beneath a strike

Sulphur *March Brown*

Hatch matching nymphs such as these Eastern March Brown and Sulphur nymphs often share the same general form. But by changing materials, material colors, and hook sizes you can imitate many different mayflies.

ndicator (a fancy term for a fly fishing bobber) are similar to learning to fish a spinning rod with bait and a bobber, techniques so simple that most children catch their first fish this way. This is not meant to somehow degrade nymph fishing. The fact that basic nymphing techniques are so effective and easy to learn should be seen as a positive. And there are also more advanced nymphing techniques, beyond this book's scope, that certainly elevate the method well past the beginner stage.

Nymph fishermen and their fly patterns can be broken into two categories: imitators and attractors. The imitator nymph fisherman studies aquatic insects, trying to replicate each type to tie the most realistic nymphs possible. Attractor fishermen carry far fewer fly patterns because they aren't trying to exactly replicate an aquatic insect. They're trying to use patterns that are just close enough to the naturals that fish won't care. Which approach is better? Perhaps it's a combination of the two methods.

There are dozens of nymph patterns that are meant to imitate specific aquatic insects. Most of these are created by simply changing material colors to best imitate the natural, though there are specific pattern that require particular materials. Some of the best nymph fishermen I know carry specific nymph patterns for important hatches, yet they fish attractor nymphs too, mostly during non-hatch periods. But it can be a great confidence builder and extremely satisfying if you take the time to have specific nymph patterns for your favorite water. Though if you do not have the inclination, time, or desire to procure so many patterns, then a great number of fish can still be caught with a smaller selection of general nymph patterns like Pheasant Tails and Hare's Ears.

Pheasant Tails

It's possible that more trout are caught on Pheasant Tails in the United States than any other nymph pattern. Most mayflies darken before they emerge, often to a dark brown color—the exact color of a Pheasant Tail. This dark brown coloration is particularly common with many mature swimmer and crawler nymphs, though burrowers and clingers also darken. Pheasant Tails are even passable imitations of Grannom caddis cases.

Pheasant Tail   Beadhead Flashback   Beadhead CDC
Pheasant Tail   Pheasant Tail

Pheasant Tails can be tied with or without beads and synthetic flash wing cases. The ones pictured here are a standard Pheasant Tail, a Beadhead Flashback Pheasant Tail, and a Beadhead CDC Pheasant Tail. These flies are some of the most commonly used nymphs around the world because they are so effective at catching fish.

| Standard Hare's Ear | Flashback Hare's Ear | Olive Hare's Ear |

Hare's Ears may be the most versatile nymph pattern. They can be dyed multiple colors, tied with or without beads, and tied slim or brushed out to imitate narrow or wide natural nymphs. Standard, Flashback, and olive-dyed above.

Hare's Ears

If the Pheasant Tail is the king of nymph patterns then the Hare's Ear may be the queen. This versatile fly pattern belongs in every angler's box. It can be tied in a wide array of colors to best imitate nymphs that aren't quite ready to emerge. For example, if I was imitating a Hendrickson hatch, I would fish olive Hare's Ears weeks before the hatch begins, and I would use brown Pheasant Tails during the hatch. With these two fly patterns anglers are able to imitate the entire span of nymph development for nearly all mayfly species.

Hare's Ear Nymphs are probably the most versatile pattern for fishing subsurface. Because hare's ear dubbing often includes natural guard hairs, it usually appears shaggy and buggy. This makes large Hare's Ears Nymphs excellent choices to imitate the huge burrowing nymphs of the many *Hexagenia* and drake species that have prominent gills along their abdomens. Yet Hare's Ears can also be tied thin, without wing cases, to imitate crane fly larvae. And a Hare's Ear tied with a flattened lead underbody may be the best option for anglers attempting to imitate the generally wide and flat form of clinger nymphs.

| CDC Beadhead Prince | Prince Nymph | Prince of Darkness |

Prince Nymphs do not imitate specific insects. They are attractor nymphs. Princes can be tied in many different colors, with or without beads. Here we have a CDC Beadhead Prince, a Standard Prince, and a Prince of Darkness.

Prince Nymphs

Most versions of Prince Nymphs share one important trait—a peacock herl body. There's just something about this shimmering, olive-green material that trout often

ind irresistible. These patterns are usually used as searching, or attractor, flies; flies that
re not intended to match a specific hatch, but rather just fished because opportunistic
rout will often eat them. But they are often fished during Eastern *Isonychia* hatches
ecause the white biots on their back looks similar to the white strip on many
sonychia nymphs. In the West, it's common to have several varieties of Prince Nymphs
n every fly shop. Most of these variations change the color of the pattern's biot wings
r maybe its body. Some replace the peacock herl with flashy synthetic materials.

With all of the possible derivations of Prince Nymphs available today, this versatile
attern is one of the most commonly fished in U.S. trout waters. I particularly like
Prince Nymphs for imitating swimming nymphs because the shimmering peacock herl
helps provide the illusion of movement.

Caddis Larva     Sparkle Pupa

The basic caddis larva nymph pattern, tied on a heavy wire scud hook, is an excellent imitator
of the worm-like caddis larva. Gary LaFontaine's Sparkle Pupa, a groundbreaking pattern in the
980s, continues to catch trout during caddis hatches across the United States.

Caddis Larva and LaFontaine Pupa

The caddis larva is perhaps the easiest of all flies to tie, and yet it catches more trout
each season than many other popular flies. These nymphs are usually tied on heavy
wire scud hooks with or without a bead head. The flies most often have tan, olive, gray,
r bright-green dubbed bodies, chosen according to the most commonly found larvae
iving in a stream or to match what is currently hatching. Sometimes a copper, gold, or
silver wire is counter-wrapped (wound the opposite direction the dubbing was wound)
o add segmentation and give the fly a little more weight and flash. Antron yarn or soft
hackle feathers can be added to make the patterns useful as caddis pupa imitators.

LaFontaine Pupa and Deep Sparkle Pupa are good choices to match the caddisfly's
upal development stage. They are important patterns to fish during all caddis
emergences, and every angler should carry a few in their fly boxes

Copper John and Stonefly Nymphs

There are dozens of stonefly nymph patterns available today. Many of them use goose
biots as their tails and often for their legs, though rubber has also become a popular
choice in recent years. Perhaps the stonefly nymph genera's most common shared traits
are its double wing cases. Though the materials used to form the cases vary, this feature

Copper John   *Double Bead Stone*

Stonefly nymphs are usually tied black, golden yellow, or olive like the Double Bead Stone pictured here, depending upon which species you are trying to imitate. The standard Copper John can be tied in the same color configurations to imitate smaller stonefly nymphs.

is obvious on real stonefly nymphs and commonly imitated by fly tiers. Black, yellow, and olive stonefly nymph patterns are most common.

Since the release of John Barr's book, *Barr Flies,* his Copper John fly pattern has become popular. These flies are attractor patterns, not really intended to imitate a specific hatch. But medium size Copper Johns tied in shades of black, brown, yellow, and olive are excellent imitators of small stonefly nymphs. The pattern's beadhead and wire body allows the flies to sink quickly to the stream bottom, exactly where trout are looking for real stonefly nymphs.

The Rubberlegs is a simple pattern that can be tied in many different colors to imitate various species of stonefly nymphs, though it is often used as a searching fly in a tandem rig with a large buoyant dry fly.

Pat's Rubberlegs

Few flies have fewer materials in their construction than the Rubberlegs. The Rubberlegs has a chenille body and rubber legs, though it often contains lead wraps beneath the chenille. But that's it. The Rubberlegs is designed to imitate stonefly nymphs, which are always available as trout food because of their lengthy (1 to 3 year) life cycle. This makes the Rubberlegs a very popular fly, particularly with Western guides and anglers, though I know some savvy Eastern anglers that fish them in smaller sizes, often on jig hooks. The Rubberlegs is very commonly fished on large, turbulent Western freestone rivers that contain large stonefly populations, such as Montana's Yellowstone, but in smaller sizes, it can also be used in similar waters in the East, particularly during periods of high or discolored water. A Rubberlegs fished below a large Chubby is a deadly combination for Western anglers during springtime and early summer fishing.

As with all stonefly nymphs, you want the flies drifting naturally along the river bottom, so make sure you're fishing them deep. You might need to add additional weight to accomplish this, and you'll know you're in the proper trout feeding zone if you are occasionally snagging the stream bottom.

Jig heads and Czech nymphs have been made popular in America due to the recent growth in competition fishing techniques in the U.S. Any fly can be tied with a jig head, just like this Flashback Pheasant Tail. But most Czech nymphs look like large caddis larva.

Euro-Nymphs and Jig Heads

International competition fishing techniques, once only popular outside the U.S., have seen tremendous growth in North America in recent years. Because these competitions do not allow anglers to use any kind of weight attached to their leaders (split shot for example), weight must be incorporated into the flies with lead wire underbodies or tungsten beads and jig heads.

European nymphing techniques often incorporate an "anchor fly" as part of a tandem nymph rig. Anchor flies are often tied to look like caddis larva and they are especially heavy to pull the tandem nymph deeper into the water column. Jig heads are also incorporated into flies to make them heavier. Jig heads also make a nymph hang from the leader at a slight angle, making the fly look a little different than those hanging straight down. Sometimes a slightly different look from a nymph pattern is all it takes to inspire a trout to eat it.

8

EAST/MIDWEST FIVE STAR HATCHES

Little Blue Winged Olive dun (male). These mayflies, often called BWOs by anglers, have a common name that describes their most obvious features: an olive colored body with a bluish colored wing. They also have two tails. But this common name is really a misnomer. Not all BWO species retain these physical traits. Body colors can range from dark olive to near chartreuse to sulphur yellow, depending upon exact species, and the chemical composition of the food it eats and the water in which it lives.

The following hatches provide some of the best fly fishing opportunities of the season. I've chosen each of them because at least two of their life stages receive a 5 ranking in Chapter 4's Hatch Progression Charts. That means that each of these hatches provides multiple fishing opportunities during their life cycle, not just at one stage, and trout usually respond by eating the naturals with gusto.

Many other hatches in the charts are worth pursuing. Any hatch that has a single stage ranked with a 4 or 5 is still a big event for most fly fishers and some with 3s, or even the occasional 2, can be worth your time. But the following hatches are the best of the best; the ones you don't want to miss.

I've made one hatch exception here; one hatch that does not meet the two-stage 5 ranking criteria—Eastern and Western Tricos. Though trout are caught each year with Trico nymph and dun patterns, their spinner stage is by far the most important and the only stage to receive a 5 ranking. But I've included Tricos in this chapter because of their extreme importance for summer fly fishing. The Trico spinnerfall is the summertime hatch king, and its fishing opportunities are too important not to be included here.

LITTLE BLUE WINGED OLIVE (*Baetis* spp.)

Little Blue Winged Olive nymphs are swimmers. They are small mayflies, with predominantly larger sizes (#18-20) appearing during the spring's initial brood and smaller ones (#20-22) in the fall. Olives often prefer to emerge during inclement weather, often on rainy, overcast days in the spring, summer, fall, and even winter on some limestone streams and spring creeks. This hatch is sometimes a snow to snow event: first appearing in early spring when winter snow is still on the ground and ending in the fall, often when the first autumn snow appears. Trout love Little Blue Winged Olives, and it's common for me to catch my first and last rising trout of the season on their dry fly imitations.

HENDRICKSON (*Ephemerella subvaria*)

Hendricksons are crawler nymphs. They look similar to Big Sulphurs in both their nymph and dun stages, and they are even similar in size. Hendricksons are one of a few mayflies whose males look different from their females. So much so that they were originally thought to be two different species. Male Hendricksons have large, prominent eyes that look like two ripe tomatoes, and their bodies are often reddish. Females look similar to female Big Sulphurs with small dark eyes and shades of olive or pink in their bodies. Hendrickson body color varies perhaps more than any other mayfly species. The Hendrickson hatch provides some of the season's most reliable fishing, often at a pleasing time of day. This hatch is sometimes referred to as the "Gentleman's Hatch" because it usually appears in the afternoon, often around 2 p.m.

Hendrickson dun (female). Hendricksons usually create the first reliable dry fly fishing of the year for Eastern anglers. These three tailed mayflies are on the larger size (about a #14) and create a beefy meal for the trout.

Grannoms are one of the caddisfly "super-hatches" and are one of the few aquatic insects that are as important in the East as they are in the West. Adults have brown and black mottled wings and greenish black bodies, though the larva have bright lime-green bodies.

GRANNOM
(*Brachycentrus* spp.)

The Grannom is the only caddis super-hatch in the East and Midwest. Anglers use the term "super-hatch" to describe those aquatic insects that hatch in extremely large numbers and produce excellent fishing opportunities. Grannom larvae are Tube-case Makers, which construct dark brown cases that look like oil derricks or ice cream cones. Grannoms have a wide size variation (12-16), depending upon the species. Their emergence often coincides with the end of the Hendricksons in the East, and it is common to find both insects on the water at the same time. There is one drawback to the extreme biomass created by a Grannom emergence: it's sometimes difficult for trout to notice your imitation among the many naturals. And trout sometimes do not rise to the adults on the surface, choosing instead to eat several of the thousands emerging subsurface.

BIG SULPHUR
(*Ephemerella invaria*)

Big Sulphur nymphs are crawlers that look similar to Hendrickson nymphs. Duns are usually size 14 to 16 and they often vary greatly in body color with some individual specimens showing yellow, orange, or olive highlights. Big Sulphurs are probably the most common mayfly species in the eastern and midwestern United States because they are able to colonize a wide range of habitats including rivers and streams that are recovering from pollution. In fact, if there are wild trout living in a stream, it probably means that the stream doesn't get too warm in the summer or completely evaporate, and it is extremely likely that that stream contains Big Sulphurs.

Big Sulphur males (dun pictured) and females look similar; however, the males have large, orange compound eyes and females have small dark-colored eyes. They both have three tails. Body colors range from deep orange to tan to yellowish with olive reflections. Wings can range from a light to a dark dun coloration.

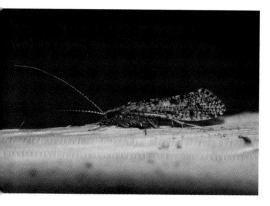

Another name for the Tan Caddis (adult, above) is the Spotted Sedge, because this insect's tan colored wings usually has darker brown spots on them. Bodies are most often a powdery tan, though some are two-toned with tan thoraxes and olive abdomens.

TAN CADDIS (*Hydropsyche* and *Symphitopsyche* spp.)

Tan Caddis are important to fly fishers not because they emerge in huge numbers, but rather they appear in good, fishable numbers for most of the season. Tan Caddis larvae are Fixed-retreat Makers that build little nets that look like spider webs along the stream bottom cobbles. They are mid-sized insects, usually size 14-18, that often have tan bodies, though in yet another common name misnomer, some "tan" caddis actually have olive abdomens. Tan Caddis larva imitations will catch fish all year, even in the winter.

LITTLE SULPHUR (*Ephemerella dorothea dorothea*)

As their name suggests, Little Sulphurs (size 16-20) look like smaller versions of Big Sulphurs (size 14-16), and just like Big Sulphurs, Little Sulphur nymphs are crawlers. It's common to find both hatches occurring simultaneously, particularly late in the Big Sulphur emergence. Little Sulphurs are less common than Big Sulphurs, but they can also vary widely in color. Little Sulphurs often occur simultaneously with Green Drakes and trout sometimes prefer the smaller Sulphurs—sometimes the best Green Drake imitation is a size 16 Sulphur.

Little Sulphur dun (male). I have found Little Sulphurs that ranged anywhere from deep orange to pale cream in color. These color variations occur because of genetic variance and as a result of diet. Wing color ranges from a bluish dun to a pale watery dun. Their three tails are often the same color as their body.

GREEN DRAKE (*Ephemera guttulata*)

The Eastern Green Drake is perhaps the most fabled of all Eastern mayflies. The burrowing nymphs live in streambed areas with fine gravel or sand. The huge Green Drakes (size 8-12) have a two-year life cycle, which means that the flies that hatch in 2016 began life as eggs in 2014. The hatch is comprised of two separate populations

Green Drakes (female dun, right) are really another misnamed fly: most of the flies are not green. There is also a lot of variance between the colorings and marking of Green Drakes in various watersheds. Some are more yellow as duns and some, almost cream. All have three tails. And all the flies turn creamy to pale white as spinners with wing venations and thorax becoming greenish black to black. The only green on the female pictured here is a slight tint to the wings.

that emerge every other year. Green Drakes get their "green" name because their wings and backs can be green colored in their dun stage. Though it's important to note that Green Drake bellies (the part the trout sees when it rises from below) are often creamy yellow, sometimes with a hint of olive. And Green Drake spinners, often called Coffin Flies, have white abdomens, though there is often a hint of yellow to the female's abdomen before she lays her eggs.

Hexagenia limbata adults. The Hex is a large mayfly, perhaps the largest mayfly of significant angler importance in North America. It is mostly a tannish yellow insect with heavily mottled wings. All of the Hex species have two long prominent tails as duns and spinners with a very small, easily missed vestigial tail between them. Courtesy of live w mcs.

MICHIGAN CADDIS (*Hexagenia limbata*)

The Michigan Caddis has one of the strangest aquatic insect common names. In fact, it may be the poster-child for why common names are completely unreliable. First, the Michigan Caddis isn't a caddis; it's a mayfly. And it's not just found in Michigan—it's actually one of the few mayfly species that can be found continent-wide.

This big (#6-8) burrowing mayfly is most important along the Great Lakes Region, though rivers, lakes, ponds, and streams throughout the Northeast and Upper Midwest can have fishable hatches. The flies often emerge in incredible numbers at dusk and well into the night, and spinner falls are also most commonly found at night. The flies, which have a two-year life cycle like Green Drakes, can bring even the largest trout to the surface to feed, making this hatch one of the most highly anticipated of the season.

Slate Drake males and females (male dun, above) look almost identical with only eye size and the appearance of a clasper, or a lack thereof, beneath their two tails to differentiate them. Slate Drake duns usually have a reddish brown to merlot colored body, though some are actually greenish when they first emerge, quickly transitioning to a more reddish appearance as they are exposed to the air. Their spinners are a deep, blood-red color.

SLATE DRAKE (*Isonychia* spp.)

Slate Drakes, like Little Blue Winged Olives, appear twice in the season—in the spring and in the fall. Their nymphs are swimmers, and they dart along the streambed like little fish. Slate Drakes seldom emerge in large numbers but trout seem to be particularly fond of them, making the hatch one of the season's best. Springtime Slate Drakes are approximately one size larger than their fall counterparts (size 12 in the spring and size 14 in the fall).

It's long been said that Slate Drakes emerge outside the water, often on streamside rocks where trout cannot reach the duns. Those who make this claim believe that any Slate Drake dun that is found on the water's surface got there by falling or being blown into the water. I believe that some Slate Drakes emerge outside the water, but I have seen others emerging in-water too. Why they emerge in two ways I do not know. But I do know that when the in-water emergers meet a trout, they are often consumed. This makes Slate Drake hatches important and fun to fish.

BROWN DRAKE (*Ephemera simulans*)

Brown Drakes have a brief emergence window, which makes them difficult to encounter for anglers with limited fishing time. Once these large flies

Brown Drake spinner (female). Brown Drakes have an over-all brownish appearance from their brown-mottled wings to their dark brown backs and three dark brown tails. But their abdomens often have an olive tint, sometimes tannish olive.

(size 10-12) begin emerging, they often last for only three or four days, and then they are done for the season. Like Green Drakes, their nymphs are burrowers, and they have a two-year life cycle, so the nymphs are present in the streambed year-round. Brown Drakes are another mayfly super-hatch capable of producing incredible numbers of insects.

Brown Drakes, again like Green Drakes, can also cause confusion with their names. Brown Drake wings and backs are shaded brown but their bellies are often a tannish olive. And it's this shade that the trout sees that should be imitated. Brown Drake spinners also have their own quirk: They tend to keep their wings upright, sometimes vibrating, as they die after mating. The upright wings can be imitated with dun patterns, rather than spent spinner imitations, but the vibrating part is a little tougher to imitate. You can try twitching hackled flies like Wulffs and Catskill-style patterns.

BLUE WINGED OLIVE (*Drunella cornuta* and *D. cornutella*)

When the Green and Brown Drake hatches are finishing for the year, a lot of Eastern anglers believe that the spring hatch season is over. But they miss some of the best dry fly fishing that will be occurring, most days, for the next week or two.

Blue Winged Olive hatches and spinnerfalls often appear in morning during warm, sunny weather near the end of the Drakes, but I have found them in the afternoon and evening too if the weather is cloudy or rainy.

Trout seem to love these size 14 and 16 mayflies, and they are fond of their strange looking spinners. The abdomens of Blue Winged Olive female spinners shrivel; this creates a chunky appearance for their thoraxes and makes their wings look over-sized. Trout become selective to these spinners, and if you are caught without a good imitation, expect a rough day. Trout rivers and streams are often getting low

Blue Winged Olive spinner (male). Blue Winged Olives (a different genus and species and not to be confused with "little" Blue Winged Olives mentioned earlier) are also often called BWOs by anglers, but their nymphs are crawlers, not swimmers. And this version of the BWO has a very bright, insect green body when it emerges. The body color quickly dulls into a more olive shade after emerging. Its wings are often a dark blue dun and it has three tails, unlike the Little BWO, which only has two tails.

and clear by the time the Olives arrive, and the fish have often been pounded for more than a week by angling hordes pursuing the legendary drake hatches. This usually makes the fish difficult to catch. You can expect trout to be rising during this hatch and spinnerfall, though catching them will test your fly patterns and fishing prowess.

Green Caddis adults usually have a mottled dark brown wing with light brown markings and a bright green body.

GREEN CADDIS (*Rhyacophila* spp.)

Green Caddis larvae are Primitive Caddisflies that look like green worms. They freely wander the stream bottom, like mayfly and stonefly nymphs, without making a case or fixed retreat. The importance of Green Caddis is similar to the Tan Caddis: Green Caddis usually do not appear in enormous numbers, but they hatch throughout a good portion of the spring, making them an important insect at the East and Midwest's best hatch-matching time of year. A bright green caddis larva imitation will work year-round in the East and is one of my favorite nymphs.

TRICO (*Tricorythodes* spp.)

Like I wrote in this chapter's introduction, Tricos are the king of summer. They usually begin hatching in July in the Northeastern United States and they continue hatching, nearly every day, until the first or second hard frost in the fall. Tricos are small (20-28) but what they lack in size they make up in biomass, sometimes dying by the thousands as they complete their life cycle. Tricos are able to colonize a wide range of habitats, included streams that are degraded, often by poor farming practices.

Male Tricos hatch at night and await the females' morning emergence. Weather dictates when Trico females emerge. Generally, the warmer the weather the earlier in the morning the females will appear. Summer emergences can occur as early as just after sunrise but the cooler days of autumn bring later hatches, sometimes as late as

Trico spinner (male). Trico nymphs are crawlers and their duns have three tails. Male bodies are brownish-olive and females are pale olive. Wings are usually pale grey, and they have no hind wing. Spinners turn dark but females maintain a cream colored abdomen.

noon. When most anglers are talking about the Trico hatch what they really mean is the spinner fall. At times Trico nymph (classified as crawlers) and dun patterns can be effective, but the hatch's climax comes each day after the males and females mate and fall spent to the water. This often inspires trout to rise in slow pools and areas outside riffles.

9

WESTERN
FIVE STAR HATCHES

Blue Winged Olive dun (male). Most Western Blue Winged Olives (BWO) look just like their Eastern counterparts with two tails, a blue dun wing, and an olive body. Blue Winged Olives are perhaps fly fishing's most important hatch; wherever you find trout fly fishermen—East, Midwest, or West—they are familiar with these insects.

Eastern trout stream hatches often receive more attention than hatches on Western streams, but that is a mistake. It's true, some days, on some Western rivers, exact imitation of aquatic insects is relatively unimportant. After all, there are often so many trout in some Western rivers that it's possible to find cooperative fish by just using attractor dry flies or nymphs. But at other times, especially during heavy, five-star hatches, it's just as important to properly imitate the natural in the West as it is in the East. This is particularly true if you want to catch specific rising trout.

BLUE WINGED OLIVE (*Baetis* spp.)

Both Eastern and Western BWO hatches are the same genus and often even the same species--though not always. Like their Eastern counterparts, Western Blue Winged Olive nymphs are swimmers, and they hatch in the rivers and streams nearly all year. They are similar in size to the Eastern olives (#16-22) and every bit as important to fly fishermen. They are particularly significant in spring creeks and tail waters, but just about every Western trout stream contains a Blue Winged Olive population.

Look for fish rising to the duns and spinners in slow water pools and glides. The spinners lay their eggs on the stream bottom and then float back to the surface where they are happily received by trout.

The Mother's Day Caddis is one of spring's most eagerly anticipated hatches, though it is sometimes diminished by higher water flows during years with early run-off. Grannom biomass can be awe-inspiring as the caddisflies hatch and lay their eggs, filling back-eddies and areas of slack current with thousands of their bodies, and creating excellent feeding opportunities for trout.

GRANNOM
(*Brachycentrus* spp.)

The size 14 to 18 Western Grannom is known by several names, because it's really comprised of two related, but different, species: one in the spring near Mother's Day and another in the late summer, which is also called the Black Caddis. To make things even more confusing, the late summer Black Caddis, or Grannom, is also known as the American Grannom because its species name is *B. americanus*. The spring Grannom (*B. occidentalis*), or Mother's Day Caddis, receives its name because it hatches in the beginning of May.

These Grannom species combine to create one of the West's most famous caddis hatches. This is unlike Eastern Grannoms where different species can overlap, but they form one hatch that occurs at roughly the same time in the spring. Both the Western and Eastern Grannom share the same genus, *Brachycentrus*. In Western rivers and streams where it occurs, the Grannom is a super-hatch and one of the most anticipated of the season.

SALMONFLY (*Pteronarcys californica*)

If the Green Drake is the most mythologized hatch in the East, then surely its Western counterpart is the

The Salmonfly is eagerly anticipated and followed with near obsession by some anglers who have heard stories (or seen it for themselves) of amazing fishing that these giant stoneflies can instigate.

Salmonfly. These giant stoneflies, size 2-12, even influence vacation time for some anglers as they try to meet the hatch's arrival. The problem with this hatch, all hatches really, is that there is no sure bet as to when they'll begin to emerge. And they don't care when you take your vacation.

Another concern is that some years, the Salmonfly hatch overlaps with run-off. Run-off occurs when snow and ice from the West's high mountains begins to melt. This influx of melt water creates unfishable conditions on most of the West's rivers and streams that do not flow from dams. It's possible that the famed Salmonfly hatch could come and go on your favorite trout water before run-off cessation allows you to fish it.

If water temperature and weather cooperate; if river flows are fishable and not blown-out by snowmelt; if it's early or late in the hatch progression, so the fish aren't gorged, then maybe the fishing will be epic. But maybe not.

GOLDEN STONES (*Calineuria, Hesperoperla, Doroneuria,* and *Claassenia* spp.)

Golden Stoneflies are another of the West's fundamental hatches. Just about every angler who wants to catch trout will be tying a size 4-10 Golden Stonefly nymph or dry to their leader at some point this season. These flies are so important because they prefer the swift-moving rocky stream bottoms found in so many Western trout rivers, though they live in smaller streams too. Golden Stones have a two- to three-year life cycle so their nymphs are available to trout all year.

Like most stoneflies, you don't always see a lot of the insects on the water, but trout get used to seeing the bugs trickle by them and actively search for these large meals. That makes fishing Golden Stonefly patterns effective long after emergences of the real bugs have subsided for the season.

Golden Stonefly adult. The "Golden Stone" is an angler given common name used for many species of stoneflies that all have yellow, gold, or tan body colors. They are one of Western North America's most important aquatic insects for trout fishing.

Like Yellow Sallies and Salmonflies, Golden Stones are eaten by trout in every stage of their life cycle. It's often effective to use tandem rigs with a Golden Stone dry fly imitation suspending a Golden Stone nymph pattern. Anglers who wish to just fish Golden Stone dry flies often do so by casting to streamside vegetation, or near the banks, where trout will often wait to ambush these large insects.

Yellow Sallies often hatch in prolific numbers, making them a key trout food source. The adults, depending upon species, have yellow bodies, often with deep orange abdomens and pale yellow to clear wings.

YELLOW SALLY (*Perlodidae* and *Chloroperlidae* spp.)

Yellow Sallies are another of the West's most common aquatic insects. Populations of these size 12-16, yellow-colored stoneflies can be found in nearly every water type from small mountain tributaries to large primary rivers. Yellow Sallies also have the significant characteristic of being eaten by trout in every stage of their development from nymph through egg layer. Most days, you won't find fish feeding steadily on Yellow Sallies, but trout seem to search for them, creating blind-casting dry fly opportunities for anglers aware of the hatch.

This hatch is a good example of how Eastern and Western hatches differ. There are small to mid-sized stoneflies in the East that anglers also call Yellow Sallies. But these flies are seldom important in any of the East's most famous trout waters, though they can work well in small, relatively sterile brook trout headwater streams. Remember, just because a hatch is important in one part of the country, doesn't mean that it matters elsewhere. This is why local knowledge from fly shops, the internet, or other anglers is vital.

PMD dun (female). In many ways, PMDs are the Western version of the Eastern Sulphur. PMDs with their three tails, pale dun to watery-colored wings, and yellowish to orange bodies, often tinted with olive, may be the single most important mayfly to anglers throughout the West.

PALE MORNING DUN (*Ephemerella dorothea infrequens* and similar spp.)

The Pale Morning Dun, or PMD, nymph (#14-18) is a crawler, just like the Eastern Little Sulphur, and the two mayflies (Little Sulphurs and PMDs) are actually subspecies of one another.

The most significant difference between Little Sulphurs in the eastern United Staes and PMDs is that while the Sulphur is primarily a late evening through dusk affair, PMDs (as their name suggests) can most often be found emerging in late morning through early afternoon—the perfect time for fly fishers.

PMDs are significant in most of the famous Western trout fisheries and their populations often inspire selective feeding by trout. Their long hatching duration, common occurrence, and the trout's propensity to eat them makes the PMD one of the most important Western mayflies along with Blue Winged Olives and Tricos.

SPOTTED SEDGE (*Hydropsyche* spp.)

The Spotted Sedge (#10-16) looks similar to the East's Tan Caddis. This caddisfly family even shares members of the same genus, *Hydropsyche*, in the East and West. Just like Tan Caddis, the Spotted Sedge can be found in nearly every trout river and stream in the West. Larva, pupa, and adult imitations can all be important, and anglers should always carry a selection of them when fishing any Western trout water. Though hatches are not often heavy, it's possible to find Western trout eating Tan Caddis any time from the spring through fall.

Just like the Eastern version, emergences of the Spotted Sedge seldom produce heavy, season-defining hatches like the Mother's Day Caddis, but rather they trickle-off most days, creating reliable fishing over a large portion the season.

HEX (*Hexagenia limbata*)

The Hex, or Michigan Caddis, can be important in the West, just as it is in the East. It is one of the few mayfly species that is found continent-wide. But just like the Eastern Hex, its Western counterparts are found in scattered, isolated locations, often in lakes and ponds, but in rivers too.

The giant Hex (#6-12) has a two-year life cycle. Duns often emerge in incredible numbers at dusk and well into the night, and spinners are also most commonly found at this time. Though not all Western anglers are aware of them, Hexes can be very important where they occur.

(*Hexagenia limbata*) dun (female). Giant Hex mayflies are important in Western streams where they live, but most Western streams don't have this hatch. A bit of local knowledge will help you find waters where this giant mayfly lives.

Western Green Drake dun (female). In another prime example of common name misidentification and confusion, Western Green Drakes are related to Eastern Blue Winged Olives, both in the *Drunella* genus, not Eastern Green Drakes, which belong to genus *Ephemera*.

WESTERN GREEN DRAKE
(*Drunella* spp.)

The Western Green Drake's crawling nymphs have nothing in common with the Eastern Green Drake's burrowing nymphs. Its *Drunella* genus means that Western Green Drakes are more closely related to Eastern Blue Winged Olives (*Drunella cornuta* and *D. cornutella*) than any of the Eastern drake species. In fact, all of the most famous Eastern Drakes (Brown, Green, and Yellow) have three tails as duns and the nymphs are burrowers while every mayfly nymph in the *Drunella* genus is a crawler with three tails as a dun.

Western Green Drakes (size 8-12) are larger than Eastern Blue Winged Olives (size 14-16) and perhaps that is why Western anglers bestowed the common name "Drake" upon them. Hatches often begin in late morning but afternoon emergences are also common. Nymph and dun stages are this hatch's most important to imitate, but trout will rise to Western Green Drake spinners when afforded the opportunity. If you find just a few Western Green Drakes on the surface, then it's a good idea to tie an imitation of one to your leader. Trout key on these duns and blind-casting dry imitations can often be effective.

WESTERN TRICO
(*Tricorythodes* spp.)

Western Tricos look and behave similar to Eastern Tricos. They are both crawlers. But the Western Tricos gives anglers one advantage that the Eastern version does not—size. Western Tricos can be approximately one to two sizes larger than Eastern Tricos (18-24 compared to 20-28). One size may not

Western Trico dun (female). Tricos create reliable hatch-matching opportunities on many Western rivers and streams during the summer.

seem like that much, but when you're dealing with aquatic insects that are this small, every little bit helps. In an uncommon geographical overlap, Western Tricos often begin in July, just like Eastern Tricos.

Though most anglers think of fishing the spinnerfall when they picture a Trico "hatch," the female duns that emerge each morning before the spinners appear can create some great fishing too. And you'll usually find few anglers on the water early enough to work the fish rising to female Trico duns.

Trico hatches can be famously difficult to imitate with dry flies. But my friend and hatch matching legend, Charlie Meck, often fishes a sunken Trico behind a dry fly. Trico spinners get churned subsurface as they flow through riffle after falling spent to the water. Many times, trout will eat the flies beneath the surface. One of my favorite tandems for fishing the Trico hatch is a sunken Trico spinner tied to the bend of a Tan Caddis (Spotted Sedge) dry fly.

10

OTHER IMPORTANT
TROUT STREAM FOODS

Midge larvae are often black, brown, olive, or red. Trout sometimes key on specific midge larvae colors, and there are days when the fish refuse one color altogether only to gorge themselves on another. Don't get stuck using only one favorite fly. Experiment throughout the day to see which is working best.

Though the big three aquatic insects—mayflies, caddisflies, and stoneflies—receive the bulk of attention from fly fishers, at times these glamour bugs fail to inspire trout that are feeding on the myriad of other food items in their world. Some of these items are lesser known aquatic insects. Some are terrestrials, land dwelling insects that haphazardly reach the water. But if you cannot identify and imitate these insects, you might not catch any fish that day. Every trout stream will not have every one of these food sources, but if catching fish is your goal, then it's vital for you to understand the "other" aquatic and terrestrial insects living in and along your favorite trout waters.

MIDGES (Diptera, Chironomidae)

Midges, though common in nearly all trout water, are sometimes overlooked, and often cursed, by fly anglers. As their name suggests, midges are small. Many anglers don't like to fish them because their diminutive size makes them as difficult to tie at the vise as they are to tie onto your leader, and they are difficult to see on the water. But trout sometimes love eating them.

Emerging midge adults can bring fish to the surface even in winter. You can often find them crawling along streamside snow and ice if they escape the water and fish. If you find fish rising in the winter, most of the time, they are eating midges.

I write that trout "sometimes" love to eat them because it is common for trout to ignore midges, particularly in healthy streams with a great deal of other food options. Midges are capable of living in degraded, polluted waters, so they are often one of the first aquatic insects to return as a waterway heals from pollution. They can be important in these degraded streams where trout cannot afford to be picky with their dinner options.

Anglers that love midge fishing often choose small fly rods and wispy leaders and tippets to match. They see the game of fooling a large trout on such small flies and tackle as the ultimate pursuit. Others compromise to reluctantly fish these miniscule patterns. They use a large dry fly and then trail a small floating or sinking midge larva pattern behind it, using the more visible dry fly as a strike indicator. Midge larva patterns are seldom elaborate creations. Often, red, olive, or black thread wound along the hook shank is all that is needed.

Zebra Midge   *JuJu Chironomid*   *Griffith's Gnat*

Griffith's Gnats imitate clusters of mating midges, allowing them to be tied larger than a single midge and making them easier to see. Zebra Midges are excellent subsurface imitations of midge larvae and pupae. Jumbo JuJu Chironomids are effective midge larva imitations for stillwater fisheries.

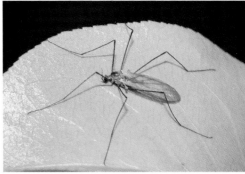

As their name suggests, giant crane fly larva like this one are big (#6-10 hook). But most crane flies are smaller, about the size of a 12 or 14 nymph hook. Crane fly larvae are an excellent source of protein for the fish and trout eat them in most rivers and streams throughout North America.

Crane fly adults look similar to mosquitoes. Most of their body mass is low calorie wings and legs, so they are often times ignored by the fish. But I have witnessed trout actively eating crane fly adults, most commonly on degraded streams with fewer food options.

CRANE FLIES (DIPTERA, TIPULIDAE)

Crane flies look like mosquitoes to most people. They have the same long thin legs, wings held at rest over their backs, and thin segmented bodies. But most important for fly anglers, crane flies can't bite us, but trout like to bite them.

Crane flies are most readily available to trout as larvae where they look similar to inchworms, though some giant crane flies are quite large and look more like pale, hairless caterpillars. Trout will eat crane fly adults, particularly in degraded rivers and streams where fish tend to be less choosy. I have seen heavy crane fly emergences and egg laying events in fertile, healthy waters where the naturals were clearly ignored by trout. And I have seen sparse hatches on degraded waters where every fish seemed to key on crane fly adults and imitating them determined success or failure. There aren't a lot of calories in the adults, which are mostly legs and wings. But a juicy crane fly larva imitation can often catch trout even in the best, most prolific fisheries. Though there are specific, and sometimes even complicated, patterns for imitating crane fly adults, simple parachute dry flies or Catskill spider patterns work well. For imitating the larvae, a Walt's Worm or tan caddis larva will usually catch fish.

Though you can tie specific flies to imitate crane fly larvae and adults, a parachute-style dry fly and Walt's Worm can also get the job done.

Dragonfly nymphs can be a very important trout food in rivers and streams throughout the country. Nymphs are much more important as a trout food option than the adults that seldom end up in the water.

Dragonfly adults are predators themselves, eating other aquatic insect adults like mayflies and caddisflies. While they may be occasionally eaten by trout, as a general rule they are not common fare.

DRAGONFLIES AND DAMSELFLIES (Odonata)

Dragonflies and damselflies are not often considered important insect species for trout fishing in the eastern United States. This is probably because stillwater trout fisheries, where the insects are often found, are not always highly regarded in parts of this region. But these insects can also be found in rivers and streams in the East and trout do eat them, particularly their larval or nymph stages. Western fly fishermen seem to have a higher admiration for these flies, which is probably due to their greater appreciation of stillwater fisheries.

Damselflies and dragonflies have complete life cycle like caddis. Nymphs can be slowly stripped along the stream bottom or quickly pulled toward the surface. During heavy hatches, trout will sometimes selectively feed on adults that are blown or fall to the surface. This is a great time to explore a pond or lake with some type of watercraft like a pontoon boat, casting dry fly imitations to rising fish.

Foam Damsel

Repunzal

Hare's Ear

An olive Repunzal is a good representation of a damselfly nymph, but I like Hare's Ears dyed olive for imitating dragonfly nymphs. Strip the flies to imitate the natural's swimming motion. Adult dragonflies are not often eaten by trout. But a Foam Damsel is a good imitation for trout eating damselflies on the surface.

Damselfly nymphs are often eaten in stillwater environments—lakes and ponds—where they can be very important to imitate if you want to catch fish. Strip fly patterns slowly with occasional twitches to imitate the way in which the insects move through the water.

Unlike dragonfly adults, it's common to see trout feeding on damselfly adults in lakes and ponds. Damselflies seem to spend more time holding on to plants near the water where they are blown or fall into the water giving the fish increased opportunities to eat them.

Aquatic worms are found in nearly every trout stream. They look similar to the earthworms in your back yard and fish love them. A large number of fly patterns imitate aquatic worms, but the most common is the San Juan Worm.

Pig Sticker   Wire Bodied San Juan   Beaded San Juan

Worm patterns are excellent choices when the water is running high and/or off-color.

AQUATIC WORMS (Annelida Oligochaeta)

Aquatic worms are not one of the glamour insects for hatch matching specialists. In fact, some anglers refuse to tie a San Juan Worm onto their leader because they look down upon the insects as little more than bait. Aquatic worms look similar to common earthworms, but they live in the stream bottoms of most trout fisheries.

One of the best times to fish an aquatic worm pattern is after a heavy rain. Two things happen when waters rise after rain: Current increases and clarity diminishes. Both of these conditions aid the use of brightly colored aquatic worm imitations. Trout are much more easily fooled by our fly pattern if they fail to get a good look at them. So if the water is moving more quickly than normal with a little color from run-off, then a trout is more likely to believe that a bright red San Juan Worm is the real thing.

The increased current after heavy rain does another thing to increase the effectiveness of worm patterns: It dislodges real ones that live in the streambed. Though some earthworms may also get washed into a stream after heavy rain, it's much more likely that worms that are already living in the stream have become more accessible to trout because increased current has set them adrift.

SCUDS (AMPHIPODA) AND SOW BUGS (ISOPODA)

Scuds and sow bugs aren't really aquatic insects. They are crustaceans, more closely related to shrimp than mayflies. But I've included them here because they are often important for catching trout. Both tend to live near aquatic plants, and though scuds and sow bugs are often found in clean and healthy streams, the presence of sow bugs can actually be an indicator of water pollution.

Scuds are good swimmers that are usually tan, olive, or gray colored. It's common for one color can be more common than others in a particular stream, so it's best to study the scuds in the waters you fish to choose the best color for your fly patterns. But most scuds turn orange when they die and orange fly patterns catch fish too.

Sow bugs are poor swimmers that are usually gray in color. Sow bugs are most often found crawling around areas of submerged vegetation. Both scud and sow bug fly patterns are most often fished drag-free beneath an indicator, though slowly stripping scud patterns can also be effective.

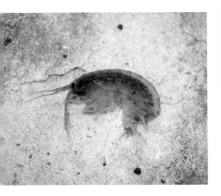 

Scuds, also known as freshwater shrimp, can be different colors in different streams with olive, tan, or gray being the most common (though they often turn orange when they die).

Sow bugs are usually gray and they look very similar to the little pill bugs you see crawling beneath rotting logs in the forest. They are most commonly found within submerged aquatic weed beds.

Scud patterns can be olive, tan, gray, or orange. Sow bug fly patterns (far right) are usually tan or gray.

HELLGRAMMITES AND DOBSONFLIES, FISHFLIES, AND ALDERFLIES (*MEGALOPTERA*)

HELLGRAMMITES AND DOBSONFLIES, FISHFLIES

If you could give stoneflies an attitude and the ability to chomp a human finger then they would become a member of Megaloptera. Not all the insects in this family are large or bite, but some like Dobsonflies (adult form of the Hellgramite) and Fishflies are big insects and they will. These insects are much more important and commonly found in the East than in the West.

Fishfly adults look like slightly smaller versions of Dobsonflies. They both have four down wings that look similar to stonefly adult wings, no tails, grayish-brown segmented bodies and fierce looking mandibles. But, in addition to the size variation, adult Fishfly adults have white stripes across their wings, which Dobsonflies and stoneflies do not have. Fishfly and Hellgramite larvae also look similar with long, segmented bodies that are lined with projections that look like legs. Unlike Fishflies, Hellgrammites have gills between these appendages on their abdomens.

Fishfly larvae look similar to Hellgrammites. but Fishfly larva do not have prominent gills beneath their appendages. Fishflies are more commonly found in cool trout waters than Hellgrammites, which prefer warmer water.

Fishfly adults are only occasionally eaten by trout, but you should have an imitation or two in your fly box just in case. Their smaller size and white markings on their wings make them easy to distinguish from Dobsonflies, which look similar.

Imitating Dobsonflies or adult Fishflies with dry flies is seldom effective. I'm not positive that I've ever seen a trout eat a Dobsonfly. Perhaps they are simply not often available to trout as adults. Dobsonflies lay their eggs on streamside vegetation where the larva then hatch and drop or crawl into the water. But my friend Charlie Meck has a good imitation of a Fishfly adult that he uses in tandem with a small nymph, and he has caught trout on the dry fly. So trout probably do eat the occasional adult Fishfly.

The most important part of the Dobsonfly and Fishfly life cycle, for the fly fisher, is their larval stage. Try slowly stripping a black or dark gray Woolly Bugger along the stream bottom or dead drift them beneath a strike indicator through areas of the stream with current.

The Hellgrammite (larva) is the most important part of the Dobsonfly life cycle for trout fishing in the few places where the two overlap. A black or gray Woolly Bugger is an excellent imitation.

Dobsonfly adults are usually not important to imitate. Their females lay eggs on streamside vegetation, keeping them from dying on the water where trout can eat them.

Alderfly larvae are much smaller than Dobsonfly or Fishfly larvae, but they still have the leg-like appendages along their abdomens indicative of Megaloptera species.

Alderfly adults look similar to caddisfly adults but lack the fine hairs along their bodies and wings that make caddis adults buoyant. This lack of buoyancy makes fishing a drowned Alderfly adult pattern worthwhile.

ALDERFLIES

Alderflies are the lesser-known cousin to Dobsonflies and Fishflies. Alderflies look similar to Black Caddis with their black antennae and dark-colored wings held folded over their body. But Black Caddis are smaller and covered with fine hairs, and the Alderflies are smooth. And for fly fishers, there is a significant difference for imitating these two insects. Caddis adults float, making them ideal fodder for surface feeding trout. But adult Alderflies lack the hairy fibers that trap air, allowing caddis to float, so adult Alderflies often times sink more quickly when they fall or are blown into the water, though they can sometimes be found floating in flat pools before riffles churn them subsurface.

Alderfly larvae are peculiar looking insects. Their bodies are orange and the rounded shape of their head resembles Black Caddis (*Chimarra* spp.) larvae. But the projections on both sides of their abdomen look similar to the other Megaloptera species. An orange caddis larva imitation is an acceptable pattern to match Alderfly larvae.

The most important Megaloptera fly pattern is a standard black Woolly Bugger tied in various sizes. Make sure the flies are heavily weighted to ride along the streambed. Fish them dead drift or slowly strip them along the bottom.

Grasshoppers inadvertently fly or jump into trout water making them an easy meal for fish. Though they are more important in the West, grasshopper imitations are also good summertime searching patterns in Eastern waters.

TERRESTRIALS

Terrestrials are not aquatic insects; they are born, and live, on land. Because terrestrials do not originate in the water, they must somehow reach the water for fish to have a chance to eat them. And trout do love to eat them, making terrestrials an important piece of any trout fisherman's arsenal.

In the West, amazing numbers of grasshoppers emerge on the valleys and plains and are blown by heavy winds across wide expanses and into the great trout rivers like Montana's Yellowstone. Eastern states' geographies are more tightly compacted with weathered mountain chains that give the terrain a more claustrophobic feel. Winds do not gather the momentum they way they do in the West, so hopper fishing is less important. But there are still many trout caught by Eastern anglers using hopper imitations because some grasshoppers do find their way into Eastern trout waters.

These insects use the method that many other terrestrials use to get within a trout's reach: they accidentally fall or jump into the water. Ants, flying ants, beetles of all sizes and colors, inchworms, moths, caterpillars, and cicadas can all find themselves as a late spring, summer, or early fall meal for a trout. But terrestrial fishing will continue to be productive for a short time after autumn's first or second frost kills all of the real bugs.

It's not common to find hundreds of terrestrials on the water with trout rising to them in a steady rhythm. But it can happen. Colonies of flying ants can sometimes

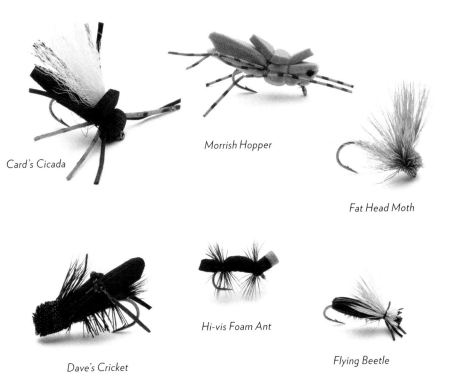

Card's Cicada

Morrish Hopper

Fat Head Moth

Dave's Cricket

Hi-vis Foam Ant

Flying Beetle

Trout love terrestrials, and fly patterns incorporating both natural and synthetic materials will catch trout from coast to coast.

cover the water. And when periodical cicadas appear by the hundreds of thousands, the trout can put on a show that is not to be missed. But these events are exceptions to the rule. Most of the time, anglers will be blind-casting terrestrial patterns to likely trout-holding spots near vegetation and hoping for the best.

Generally speaking, it's not important to carry a vast array of terrestrial patterns. But it's wise to have a couple diverse imitations for popular, long lasting terrestrial fishing opportunities like the West's hopper fishing or ants and beetles in the East. Most anglers think of dry fly fishing when they think of terrestrials, and foam fly patterns that incorporate flashy, synthetic materials are popular. But terrestrials using deer hair like Crowe Beetles and deer hair ants and inchworms still work well. Most terrestrial patterns fished on the surface should be cast with a gentle plop near streamside vegetation where an insect could accidentally fall into the water.

Though floating terrestrial patterns are the most commonly used, they are not the only way to catch trout. After terrestrials fall or get blown into the water, they begin to tumble through riffles and eventually drown. These drowned insects will be swept

Aquatic beetles and true bugs, like backswimmers, can be important trout food sources in some fisheries. They are most often imitated by Western stillwater anglers, but trout eat aquatic beetles in rivers and streams throughout North America.

by currents along the streambed and taken subsurface the same way a mayfly nymph would be eaten, making sunken terrestrial patterns effective. Because you're imitating dead insects with sunken terrestrials, it's usually best to fish them drag free, the same speed as the current, and along the stream bottom. This is a good time to fish a dry fly with a sunken fly underneath it.

To fish this tandem, attach an 8- to 18-inch piece of tippet with a clinch knot (you want the sunken fly floating near the stream bottom so the exact length will be determined by the water's depth) to the bend of a dry fly's hook that is tied to your leader. Then tie the sunken terrestrial pattern to the tippet. It's a good idea to use a highly visible and buoyant dry fly so you can see it easily if a fish eats the sunken terrestrial. A cricket or grasshopper pattern works well for this. The dry will hesitate, move upstream, or sink when the sunken terrestrial is eaten.

The following chart examines the importance of trout stream insects that aren't from one of the big three groupings: mayflies, caddisflies, and stoneflies. The chart works on a comparative rating scale from 1 to 5. A ranking of 1 means that the insect is of very little importance and that the angler should not bother imitating it. A 5 ranking means that the insect is of widespread importance throughout the region, or water type, and that it should definitely be pursued and imitated with the suggested type of fly. The rankings are comparative, meaning that if the insect receives a 5 ranking for dry flies and a 2 ranking for nymphs, then it is more important for the angler to imitate this insect with dry flies; though nymphs can still be of occasional, but much lesser, effectiveness.

To further explain, let's examine the entry for Dragonflies and Damselflies. They have received a 2 rating for Eastern importance and a 4 for Western importance. This means that the insects are significantly more important to Western fly fishers than Eastern anglers. The 3 rating for dry fly importance means that anglers can expect to catch some fish with dry fly imitations, but the 5 rating for nymphs means that you're more likely to have success fishing sunken versions of these flies. They receive a 5 rating for stillwaters meaning that this is the best type of water to find these insects and fish eating them. Their 2 ratings in freestone, tailwater, and spring creek waters means that though they may be found in these habitats in smaller numbers they are much less important in these habitats than they are in stillwaters.

Stripping damselfly nymph imitations fooled this big rainbow on Wyoming's Monster Lake.

Chart IV: Other Insect Importance Chart

Insect	Eastern/ Midwest	Western	Imitated with Dry Flies	Imitated with Nymphs
Midges	5	5	5	5
Craneflies	4	2	2	5
Dragon and Damsel Flies	2	4	3	5
Aquatic Worms	5	5	1	5
Scuds and Sowbugs	5	5	1	5
Megaloptera	3	1	2	4
Ants	5	5	5	4
Flying Ants	5	5	5	3
Terrestrial Beetles	4	4	4	1
Hoppers	3	5	5	1
Crickets	3	3	5	1
Inchworms and Caterpillars	3	2	3	3
Moths	2	4	5	1
Cicadas (aka Dog Day Cicadas)	2	3	5	1
Periodical Cicadas	5	2	5	2
Aquatic Beetles	2	4	1	5

Insect	Stillwaters	Freestones	Tailwaters	Spring Creeks and Limestone Streams
Midges	5	4	5	5
Craneflies	3	3	3	4
Dragon and Damsel Flies	5	3	2	2
Aquatic Worms	2	5	5	5
Scuds and Sowbugs	2	2	4	5
Megaloptera	1	3	2	2
Ants	3	5	5	5
Flying Ants	3	5	5	5
Terrestrial Beetles	1	4	3	5
Hoppers	1	5	4	5
Crickets	1	4	3	4
Inchworms and Caterpillars	1	3	3	4
Moths	1	4	4	3
Cicadas (aka Dog Day Cicadas)	1	4	3	2
Periodical Cicadas	3	5	5	5
Aquatic Beetles	4	2	2	3

11

RESOURCES

———

For more detailed information about aquatic insects, I recommend the following:

Books for Eastern and Midwestern Hatches
Pocketguide to Pennsylvania Hatches, Charles Meck and Paul Weamer
Pocketguide to New York Hatches, Paul Weamer
The Hatches Made Simple, Charles Meck
Caddisflies, Thomas Ames
Hatches II, Al Caucci and Bob Nastasi
Caddisflies, Gary LaFontaine
Selective Trout, Doug Swisher and Carl Richards

Books for Western Hatches
Pocketguide to Western Hatches, Dave Hughes
Hatches II, Al Caucci and Bob Nastasi
The Hatches Made Simple, Charles Meck
The Complete Book of Western Hatches, Rick Hafele and Dave Hughes
Caddisflies, Gary LaFontaine
Selective Trout, Doug Swisher and Carl Richards

Websites (For East, Midwest, and West)
Troutnut: Aquatic Insect Encyclopedia: www.Troutnut.com
Purdue University's Mayfly Central: www.entm.purdue.edu/mayfly/
Fly Fishing Entomology: www.flyfishingentomology.com
Trichoptera World Checklist:
www.clemson.edu/cafls/departments/esps/database/trichopt/

The author with a beautiful cutthroat trout caught in Yellowstone National Park.

ABOUT THE AUTHOR

Paul Weamer is a *Fly Fisherman* magazine contributing editor and the author or co-author of several fly fishing books. He is an accomplished photographer, specializing in aquatic insect macro photography, and has contributed photos to *Fly Fisherman*, *The Catskill Regional Guide*, and *The Drake*, as well as his own and several other writer's books. Paul is a former licensed guide, working the Upper Delaware and Beaverkill Rivers for trout and smallmouth bass, and Cattaraugus, Elk, and Walnut Creeks for steelhead. He has owned or managed three highly regarded fly shops in New York and Pennsylvania and has been a production tier for numerous guides and shops, including the legendary Dette fly shop in Roscoe, New York. Paul is a contract fly designer for the Montana Fly Company and the inventor of the Weamer's Truform, Comparachute, Alewife, Bucktail Body, and the Weamer Streamer series of flies.

Paul is one of the founders of the Friends of the Upper Delaware River (FUDR), and is a current member of the Outdoor Writers Association of America. He was the 2009 co-winner of FUDR's Upper Delaware "One Bug" tournament and winner of the 2011 Upper Delaware Council's Recreation Award for his book about the river. Paul is a Pro Staff member for Simms and Orvis, as well as Regal Engineering and Daiichi hooks where he designed the Daiichi #1230, Weamer's Truform Mayfly Hook.

In 2014 Paul and his wife, Ruthann, moved to Livingston, Montana, where Paul works for Sweetwater Fly Shop and continues to design flies, shoot photographs, and write books and magazine articles.